BEST SEAT IN THE HOUSE

Suddenly Quadriplegic, Now What?

THE DAVID VAN GORDER STORY

Carol Tanko

LIVES FOREVER CHANGED PUBLISHING
PRESCOTT, ARIZON

ISBN 979-8-4534-1952-4

Book design by Longworth Creative, LLC
www.LongworthCreative.com

First Edition
Printed in the United States of America

This book is dedicated to David Van Gorder. He was the love of my life. He was also the kindest, most grateful man I have ever met. He was fun and funny, wise and silly, brave, and thoughtful. David has been an inspiration to me and to everyone he counted as a friend— he counted everyone as his friend. It is my hope that by putting his challenges and successes on paper, he will continue to be a friend and an inspiration to you.

– Mary, with Love

CONTENTS

ACKNOWLEDGEMENTS

From the deepest part of my heart and all the gratitude I can express, I thank all of our friends, neighbors, relatives, and life acquaintances who have helped and supported us throughout the years. We could not have managed climbing this huge mountain of responsibility without you. The community interaction, on all levels, enabled us to feel like we were a part of the ebb and flow of a normal life. Sometimes, just feeling normal is the greatest gift of all.

David was born lucky to have Jerry as his life-long friend. Jerry is the most faithful person and loving human being David ever knew. Jerry was as interested in David's own welfare as he was in his own.

In every life there are very special people without whom we could not have succeeded to the extent we were able. Barry Cohen was one of those people. There is no way to repay his kindness and generosity. Thank you. Thank you. Thank you!

W. Mitchell encouraged David every day that he knew him. W. Mitchell opened the doors to David's mind and let solutions flow out. He walked in David's shoes and David walked in his.

A special thank you to Carol Tanko for bringing David's story to life, and to Margaret Rose Stewart for her excellence in editing. To Elise DuPuydt, Editor-in-Chief. To Ginger Nolte for her help with punctuation, and to Jana Fillbach for the final edit. To Barney Logan and Chuck Tanko for the title. It takes a village. We have a good one!

– *Mary Van Gorder*

FOREWORD

David Van Gorder was 22 years old when he was injured in an accident and became a quadriplegic. He was given 7 – 12 years to live. When he didn't progress as he had expected, he became angry and depressed. If given the opportunity, he would have taken his own life. After years of self-destructive behavior, believing he might actually live longer than expected, he made a decision to add value to the life he still had. When properly motivated, ordinary people do extraordinary things. David Van Gorder was one of those people. He, in turn, motivated all of us who knew him. This is his story. I hope you enjoy his journey and that it enhances your life as it has ours.

NOTE TO READERS

This book was written partially from notes David spoke into a recorder years ago. They were transcribed, word for word, by his secretary. They were not particularly in order. David liked to use very long paragraph-like sentences. Since he couldn't write, he didn't concern himself with sentence structure, complete thoughts, or punctuation.

I have patched his notes together with stories from his wife Mary, newspaper articles, interviews, and personal knowledge to bring his extraordinary life to you in Three Dimension. I have done my best.

– Carol Tanko

SPECIAL ACKNOWLEDGEMENT

I could not let this book be published without a Super Acknowledgement to my friend and neighbor, Carol Tanko. This book would never have been published if it were not for Carol.

Years ago, David would sit with a tape recorder running and he would just talk about his accident and other feelings he was experiencing. His friends would listen to his words and type them. I had a manuscript at least 2" thick of David's thoughts and feelings. One day, out of the blue, Carol said, "We need to write David's story." I said, "He already started it." I had no idea what to do with it. I gave Carol his manuscript to read, and a few days later she said she would like to write a book with my help. I was thrilled to know his story would be told!

Carol was relentless in our meetings and never tired of gathering new stories about David's life, my life, and our life. I cannot tell you how many times I was so overwhelmed that I thought we should pull out of the idea of a book. She said, "No, I love this!" God bless her for her hours of dedication to these wonderful memories I now have for myself, and to share with my children and grandchildren.

What a wonderful friend. I will never forget your kindness. With all my respect for your tenacity and love for your energy of life.

– Mary Van Gorder

1

THE LAST DAY I WALKED

YOU MAY HAVE A PLAN for your life, or you may just choose to wing it. Some of us, as happened to me, will take a far different and virtually uncharted path that we did not choose at all. My name is David Van Gorder and this is my story. I had been walking for 22 years. Walking just like almost everyone else. Then one day, in 1965, suddenly, surprisingly, and unbelievably, I never walked again.

I remember the very last day I walked. It was my first day back to work after my honeymoon. I got out of bed, took a shower, and remember being nervous about what the work day would bring. I put on my cut-off shorts, socks, work boots, and a sweatshirt over my JC Penny's t-shirt. It seemed very important to me at the time to have on a JC Penny's Town Craft t-shirt that was thick, and of fine quality. The kind you could wear anywhere. I considered it part of my identity to have such a good quality t-shirt.

As I picked up my lunch that Madalena, my new wife of ten days, had made for me—a cheese, bologna, lettuce, mayonnaise, and pickle chips sandwich; a pastry; and a can of soda—the smell of the brown bag brought back my grammar school days. Back then it was still okay to carry lunches to school in a brown paper lunch sack.

Opening the door of my apartment, I could feel the coolness of the early morning October air on my body. I worked on a construction crew. We did plumb-line, which was to level houses, joisting, and shooting down the walls on concrete slabs with 22 round nails and a nail gun. We were also installing foundation bolts. As a result of this type of physical work, I hit my left shin on the foundations, painfully and daily!

Walking to the parking lot, my heart skipped a beat. I smiled to myself as I walked toward my 1955 Ford pick-up. I had wanted one for years. I had put so much time and energy into that little pick-up. I worked all summer to make enough money to take it to Tijuana to install a $500 Diamond Tuck upholstery. It was a popular style at the time. I put a cover over the back where I kept my tool box. My pick-up was a bright, shiny, soft orange color with chrome wheels and white walls. I loved that truck. When I opened the door and stepped into it, I could feel the coolness of the leather seat touching my legs; my back touched the diamond button tuck. When I closed the door, it had a certain metallic sound to it, but it was tight. There were no rattles. It had running boards with rubber strips on them. I could smell a hint of leather mixed with the previous days smell of cigarettes, because I smoked in those days. To the left of the large steering wheel was a button I used to turn on the ignition. Then I had to push in the clutch. It was a three-speed stick shift, and as I started it, I could feel the pressure of the clutch on my left leg and foot, even through my heavy work boots. It would just turn over a couple of times and then—bam! It would fire. I would shift it down into first and rev it a couple of times because I liked the sound of the 18" glass pack pipes. It was everything I ever wanted when I was in high school. I got my car when I was 17 ½. My parents picked it out. They put a little 6-cylinder engine in it because they knew they couldn't trust my reckless behavior. To compensate, I made it one of the most beautiful little trucks by giving it a new paint job and keeping it very clean. While driving to work that morning, I thought to myself that I had a lot going for me. I have a nice wife. We had a nice life. She had a good job as a secretary, I had the truck I always wanted.

As I shifted into gear and moved toward Nordhoff Boulevard in Canoga Park, the San Fernando Valley part of Southern California, I was looking forward to having my first dinner at home with my parents since getting married. We were going to have my favorite meal, spaghetti and a lemon meringue pie for dessert. No one made lemon meringue pie like my mom, Marge.

I was approaching Balboa Street. I was working at the end of Balboa and had been for the last five or six months. We were building tract homes in a higher-class area. I felt my truck toss me around as I pulled onto the dirt road leading to the site. No seatbelts yet in 1965! It was almost 7:00 a.m., our starting time, and others on the crew were already gathering. We all did piece work, which means we got paid by the job not by the hour. It was illegal, but I wanted, and needed, the job. I also wanted to stay in construction and validate myself as a "real man." I wanted to prove that I could handle construction work, and I was determined to learn to do it. This was important to me on another level. I was fired, not once, but twice, by my boss, John, on my first day on the job! I fell off a ceiling joist but still had the good sense to land on my feet. The second time I got fired that day was because John noticed I didn't know how to swing a hammer! I was a big strapping guy. I LOOKED like I should be able to swing a hammer. He had no idea I couldn't use a power saw either. I don't know how I talked John in to keeping me on the crew. I must have had some power of persuasion even then. And I liked working in the sun. I couldn't imagine being inside all day. I definitely was the rugged, outdoor type. Yes, construction would be just fine for me.

This might be a good time to mention that I was raised in a Christian Science family. My parents did not go to doctors. I was raised fearing doctors, medicine, shots, needles, stitches, even band-aids. I was afraid of doctors and hospitals and, therefore, of getting hurt. There were just some things I couldn't understand: How the Holy Spirit could heal without the skills of a surgeon. I didn't want to put that to a test. I didn't understand how I could be healed through the spiritual knowing of the connection that we have in every cell of our body as Deepak Chopra and my parents fervently believed. As a kid, I didn't participate in a lot of perceived dangerous activities because I feared I would be hurt. If I got hurt, I might have to go to a doctor; and now you can see my dilemma. No contact sports for me. I played the accordion for six years for heaven's sake! What could go wrong there? On the job, I was still a little boy afraid of being hurt, but I kept it to myself. Even though I tensed up each time a saw a circular saw, I was determined to conquer my fears. I would become a real, fearless man, like the other guys.

While working that day, I was thinking again of the spaghetti dinner with my wife, parents, and my brothers Bob and Jim. I might arrive home before my wife, take a shower, and perhaps we could make love before we left for dinner. So, at about 4:00 or 4:30, I walked out to my truck, took off my apron, and put my hammer away. John walked up behind me and said, "Before you go, we want to put a porch beam on this house over here." He was paying me, and I never knew how to say no, especially to someone whom I admired and thought of as a fine man's man. If you haven't noticed yet, I was trying to form an opinion and a persona of what a real man was—brave, strong, gruff, afraid of nothing!

Reluctantly, I put my apron back on and walked over to the construction site. Jim Boyd, who worked with John, was there along with a young apprentice by the name of Preacher who also did joisting jobs. He asked me to get up on the plates to install the 8'x16' porch beam. Every time I climbed up onto a high beam, I was nervous, and my stomach was in my throat knowing that I could be hurt. I had already fallen off a two-story building and a one-story building and I had not been hurt. Standing on the plates, I dropped the beam into place and nailed it down. I turned to make a teasing gesture towards John who was standing below. John, jokingly, started throwing nails at me. I picked a nail out of my apron and threw one back at him. Then, he got even more intense and wanted to shake the wall on which I was standing. He picked up a dirt clod, twice the size of his head, pitched it back over his 6'3" frame, and flung it at the wall, aiming just below my feet.

I watched, as if in slow motion. I knew there was something wrong. It was a surrealistic experience. As I watched this dirt clod coming toward me, I knew it wasn't going to hit the wall. It was headed for my feet! As it hit my legs—on my shin, where I always bumped it—the clod knocked my feet free from the wall. As I started to go over backward, I instinctively knew that I couldn't compensate like I had done twice before when I had fallen off roof joists. As I looked at the ground over my left shoulder, in that split second, I knew I was in trouble. I felt and heard a crunch and thud in my neck as it snapped. It was so loud, it hurt my ears when it happened. As I lay there on the ground looking up at the sky, trying to breathe, and trying to process what had just happened, a numb feeling crept over me. I knew that something was terribly wrong. I heard the crew laughing and joking in the background, and then they stopped. It became eerily quiet as the men came closer and gathered around me. I was on my back looking up. I said, "Please, please just lift me up. Just let me walk, I need to walk." My stomach and my chest felt compressed, and my breathing was starting to become more difficult. Later, I was told that someone who has had an injury this high up in their neck usually couldn't breathe on their own and would have needed an emergency tracheotomy or they would choke to death. As I tried to look toward my arm on my left side, I could hardly move my head. The only thing I could move was my left arm that was now down by my side. As I slid my arm across the dirt, it didn't feel like it belonged to me anymore. It was dead and it was numb. I could hear the gravel scrape under it like a carcass being dragged across the earth after it had been killed and the life had gone out of it. I was sick to my stomach. My fear and shock increased as I became more and more panicked. Two people knelt beside me. One of them said, "It's OK, just lie there. You might have the wind knocked out of you." Instinctively, I knew it was more than that, but I was hoping they were right about the wind being knocked out of me. I had never had the wind knocked out of me, so maybe this was exactly what it felt like.

There was a cut on my shin from the massive dirt clod smashing into me. It was bleeding badly, but I couldn't feel it. John noticed it and fetched up some water. He walked over and just threw it on my leg. I didn't move. I didn't even flinch. I was stiff. Now, it was John who panicked. As he ran to his truck, he shouted back over his shoulder that he was going to get an ambulance. As I lay there, seemingly forever, unmoving, looking at the shadows from the trees overhead moving across my face, I knew it had to be 5:30 or 6:00 o'clock. Still no word of help. I was getting dizzy. I believe that I started to move into shock. More people from the area began to gather around wondering what had happened.

Finally, after what seemed like an absolute eternity, the ambulance came. As I am re-living this moment, I am having feelings of burning in my face and in my eyes because the sadness never goes away. Later, I learned that the ambulance driver had a difficult time finding me at our worksite because it was such a large development. The roads were unnamed, rough with uneven dirt, making them difficult to navigate. They were doing their best in a difficult situation, as were many other caregivers I would encounter on my healing journey.

As I lay on the ground, the paramedics (they weren't actually paramedics back then, just transporters) gently put me in a neck brace and lifted me onto a gurney, setting me in the back of the ambulance. As I looked up at the ceiling one of the men sat with me, while the driver drove as slowly as he could. Every bump the ambulance took felt like someone was shoving an ice pick into both sides of my neck. At this point, I still didn't require any air, and I was completely conscious. As we turned onto Nordhoff, heading to the hospital, I asked where they were taking me. The man said, "To Holy Cross Hospital." I kind of knew where it was, but I had never been inside or seen the inside of any hospital as a patient, ever. I had only visited the nursery in the maternity ward to see a friend's newborn baby. I had been uncomfortable enough with that.

2

HOLY CROSS HOSPITAL

As THEY TOOK ME OUT of the ambulance and wheeled me into the x-ray room, I was scared. By then, my family knew I wasn't coming home for dinner. I asked the x-ray tech what happened, and he said, "You probably just knocked the wind out of yourself." He was from the mid-west, and he told me of a time he remembered when he was thrown out of a pick-up truck. He was out in the country when he slammed up against a post and was temporarily paralyzed from the shock to his spine. Later, he walked again. I hadn't had a lot of time to consider my situation, but I was hoping I might have a similar outcome. At this point, I knew something was very "not right," but everyone else seemed encouraging.

While inside the x-ray room, I experienced seeing the world from an entirely different perspective. I was lying on my back, looking up, and it occurred to me that this was one of the most helpless and vulnerable positions a person could experience. All I could see were ceiling tiles. My x-ray tech was a young guy in what looked like his early 20s. As he read my x-ray films, he carelessly said, "I don't see how a guy your size could fall completely on that spot and still be alive." Words, carelessly spoken when a person is in an extremely vulnerable situation, can have long-term and unintended consequences. This happened to me that day. Apparently, there was no hemorrhaging in the brain or clotting, for which I was thankful. But for the first time, it occurred to me how close to death I may have come, and how long it might take me to recover.

The next man I saw was a neurologist. He was a twin, one of the Mervyn brothers. He asked an orderly to shave my head so I could be put in traction. In 1965, there was really no standard of care for spinal injuries, particularly in a small-town neighborhood hospital like Holy Cross. The Mervyn brothers were well known in the Los Angeles area. But unfortunately, not for being excellent physicians! They had been sued in a libel case for negligence after Jeff Chandler, a famous Hollywood actor in their care, had the misfortune to die. Negligence was never proven, but they went through the long, drawn-out trial and gained dubious reputations among the locals. He was now my doctor. Yippee. The orderly assigned to me wasn't doing too well either. Apparently, he was more interested in his upcoming evening activities than in shaving my head! I remember Dr. Mervyn yelling at the young man to hurry along quickly. As I also remember, it was probably 3 or 4 hours before my neck was finally in traction.

By that time, my family had arrived and, unbeknownst to me, they were arguing and fighting over me in the hallway outside the neurological care ward. My parents, of whom I mentioned were Christian Science believers, wanted me removed from the hospital immediately. They were ready to take me home and hire people to pray over me. My brothers were also there. I don't know if they had an opinion or just went along with my parents. In the end, my new wife of 10 days had the final legal say, and she and my best friend Jerry determined it would be in my best interests to remain at Holy Cross under doctor's care. No matter how dubious that care might be! That decision saved my life.

Meanwhile, Dr. Mervyn had numbed both sides of my head and had drilled holes in my skull—WITH A DRILL—just like the ones on the job site! I remember feeling this mucky, cold, burning stuff on my shaved head. Bits of skin and bone had splattered on my face and cheeks. Then, I felt a clamp, very much like tongs that carry ice, being planted into the holes Dr. Mervyn had just drilled into each side of my head. The clamp, which was actually called Gardner-Wells Tongs, was being screwed down to allow them to put me into traction.

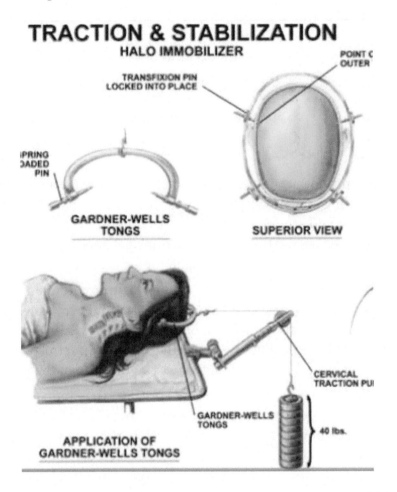

TRACTION & STABILIZATION
HALO IMMOBILIZER

POINT C
OUTER

TRANSFIXION PIN
LOCKED INTO PLACE

SPRING
LOADED
PIN

GARDNER-WELLS
TONGS

SUPERIOR VIEW

CERVICAL
TRACTION PUL

GARDNER-WELLS
TONGS

40 lbs.

APPLICATION OF
GARDNER-WELLS TONGS

Today they use halos. By using a halo, a person could be sitting up or even walking within weeks. The halo is clamped around the forehead to keep the tension off the bones and neck. But that wasn't the way it was done back then. The tongs were attached to a pully loaded with weights to pull and stretch my neck. Afterward, I was sent to ICU where I would stay indefinitely. After being in ICU a few weeks, I was told that I hadn't been able to receive phone calls because I was near death. This was news to me. At that point, I was too afraid to actually ask anyone about my prognosis. The next time a nice nurse came in (yes, there were some who were not nice or approachable), I asked her if she thought I would walk again. She said, "There's hope, there's still hope." And, so I hoped.

The nurses and orderlies had to cut every bit of clothing off of me because they couldn't move me. It took almost four days to completely clean my body since my hands, face, and everything that was exposed was completely full of dirt. I swear I looked three shades lighter. A side effect of construction, and of course, the fall!

The next thing I remember was ceilings. They were all I could see—ceilings. Eventually, when I was placed in a rotating Stryker frame, I could see floors and shoes—and my shirt! My brother was wearing my shirt! When I called him on it, he said, "Well you can't wear it anymore." He was right, for now, anyway. Just wait!

The purpose of the Stryker frame was to rotate me like a rotisserie chicken to keep pressure off my back or front. However, it was putting constant tension on my neck. Many years later, it was found to be debilitating to the lungs as well. In retrospect, it didn't make a lot of sense, but that was all they had at the time.

At one point, I was taken into surgery for a laminectomy and neck surgery. A laminectomy is a procedure that creates space by removing the lamina, the back part of a vertebra that covers your spinal canal. It is also known as decompression surgery. A laminectomy serves to enlarge your spinal canal to relieve pressure on the spinal cord and/or or nerves, whichever are being affected. The other surgery was to remove shattered bits of bone. I didn't know they were there. I never felt them. I was still in traction. My neck and head were being stretched. I knew they had given me some kind of medication because I was hallucinating. It felt like my head was being pulled off of my shoulders—and I screamed.

There was pain before the laminectomy surgery and a whole lot more afterward. The only thing I could feel was my neck, and the constant throbbing, throbbing, and more throbbing of my jugular veins, as if I was being knifed every time my heart beat. I begged my wife, or anyone who came to see me, to just put their fingers on both sides of my neck and hold them there to stop the blood flow. It gave me a few seconds of relief. The painkillers I was given weren't working, but the doctors were afraid to give me more. The pain was jaw crushing and never ending.

I shared the ICU ward with people who had all kinds of situations. Doris had a brain tumor and was in a coma. Every day, the doctor would come in, slap Doris on the foot and say, "Wake up Doris, it's me." Every day, Doris didn't wake up. I was always afraid, afraid of what would happen to Doris, afraid of what would happen to the others, and afraid of what would happen to me. No one explained anything. I was terrified and overwhelmed at being in such a foreign place, a place that my parents frowned upon. They surely thought this was the devil's own playground. Following standard practice of the day, doctors, nurses, and staff didn't tell patients what they were going to do next, or why. The procedures were a mystery, and I still didn't know what my chances of survival were, if any! Plus, there was so much incompetence among the staff as it related to me. To give them the benefit, I was an anomaly. They hadn't cared for a quadriplegic before, and no one really knew what to do with me.

Take the Stryker frame for instance. It was supposed to keep blood flowing through my body. I heard the nurses talking in the hallway. Just a side note here. I was injured, not deaf. People, since my accident, have imputed deafness to me. I don't know why. Anyway, I heard the nurses asking each other if they knew how the frame worked, how they should hook me up to it, or did they think maybe they should call someone? Thankfully, they called someone who came in on his day off and showed them how to place the platform across my forehead and keep it in place with a screw at the front top and at the front bottom. Then he taught them how to remove it from my face and move it to the plate on my back, as if I were a human sandwich. The frame then moved the patient around in a circle, not flipping them back and forth as they had thought.

At times, my arms would fall off this narrow frame, which was no wider than my shoulders. I could see them dangling there and tried with all my might to force them to make a fist, or try to pull them back on the table, to no avail. They just hung there. I used to be proud of my arms, forearms, and biceps. I worked at keeping them strong and powerful. Now, as I watched week by week, I could see they were becoming thinner, and losing their tone and strength.

This was all new to me. In retrospect, I would like to say how much my very life depended upon each and every one of the support people at Holy Cross. The routine eventually became fixed and mundane. I was never left alone. At times, all I wanted was to be left alone. On the other hand, I was too frightened to be alone and silently begged them to stay with me. If the staff hadn't been so kind, so gentle, so patient, and so vigilant, 24 hours a day, every day, I probably would not have lived to tell you my story. From the x-rays, to taking blood, looking at my neck, measuring my limbs for braces, and all the other hundreds of things for which I had not been prepared, I am grateful. I was literally being pushed, turned, checked, monitored, having my temperature taken, given tests, and inhalation therapy around the clock.

I was 22 years old and took pride in doing things for myself. I felt bad asking the nurses to come in to give me water or change the TV Channel. I hated to bother them for such small things, but I could not even ring the bell to get their attention. I had to wait until I heard someone outside my door and yell out for them to help me.

Marge was in full nurture mode, bringing me hamburgers from Bob's Big Boy to fatten me up. My dad didn't say much, and evidently, my youngest brother Jim who was four years younger, kept his own counsel. It is difficult for a seventeen-year-old boy

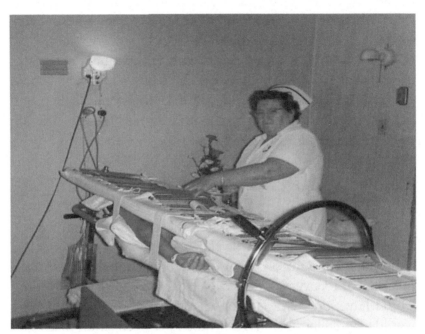

Stryker Frame

to know how to express his feelings. My other brother Bob was two years younger. He was the joker of the family. His self-appointed job was keeping the atmosphere light. My family wasn't really good at dealing with feelings. They really didn't have any comforting information either. Much like me, they didn't know if I would live from day to day, or recover, or even to what extent.

Sometimes, my father came to visit by himself. He really didn't know what to say. It was stressful for me when my parents came to visit because I felt I had to tell them everything was okay, and that I was healing. I knew he had hired a practitioner to pray for me. I was okay with that. I was willing to take all the help I could get. I constantly felt it was a betrayal to my parents' beliefs and a shaming experience for them that I was in a hospital. They, on the other hand, almost ignored the situation. There was little, if any, emotional response from them. Maybe that was their coping mechanism, or maybe they really believed that if they prayed sincerely, I would be healed.

As for me, I was also in denial. None of us, me included, knew the consequences of severing the cervical 3,4 and 5 vertebrae. So I remained in my own world of denial, hoping for any small measure of recovery. Had I ever imagined what kind of life I would have, one without hope, I know my internal structure would have collapsed. I never would have been emotionally and mentally able to retrieve myself from that kind of destruction. I stayed away from reality and acceptance of my situation for a very long time. I would have to say, even to this day as I am re-living it, I have NEVER accepted my paralysis. I have only acknowledged what I can do and what I cannot do.

One of the more pleasant sensual experiences that I waited for days to have was the simple task of taking my first shower. Every three or four days I would be helped into the shower. I couldn't feel the water, or see it, as it ran down my arms and legs, and I couldn't tell what this wet substance was that was making contact with something that I used to be able to feel as my skin.

But as the soap moved over different areas of my body, I realized I was being washed and cleaned.

In 1965 and 1966, a lot of kids I knew from high school were getting official letters from Washington commanding their presence. It was the draft. Two weeks after I had been injured and was lying in bed in the hospital, my wife brought me the day's mail. I had been drafted. At that moment, my first thought was gratefulness. I was grateful there appeared to be an opportunity for me to train as a soldier and go to Vietnam. I could exchange this hell hole I was living in for a different hell hole that I knew nothing about. As I thought those thoughts, I can honestly tell you that, at the same time, I actually believed there was a greater possibility I wouldn't come home if I were fit enough to be drafted. My name, more than likely, would be amongst the other 50,000 plus names that now appear on a wall because of a war that became a shameful part of American history.

I was feeling my own shame at the moment. I was experiencing the fact that I was currently worthless. I couldn't even fight in a conflict I knew nothing about. I was letting my country down. I was letting my wife down, just like I was letting my family and my job down.

One of the things that frustrated me most in the hospital setting was the anticipated timeline for recovery imputed to us by people very highly trained. If I didn't proceed according to a certain date or timetable, I felt they lost confidence in me and respect for me, and judged me as a failure. They felt the need to move on and away to something, or someone else. They showed no patience or respect for my individual abilities for recovery. There is a definite pattern of shock, disbelief, denial, anger, and finally acceptance that everyone experiences. Some stay in stages longer than others. Probably, professionals are better at dealing with this concept now. If you are a "superstar" and rush through all these stages, or skip any, the edges will fray sooner or later, and all these unresolved, unfinished pieces start coming apart. Timing is everything. I learned that concept in my own life.

People who had given up on me years before began to come around again. This time, I was receptive. I'm not proud of being a "hard learner," but it is what it is. Maybe it was my only way of preserving my dignity, of saying I need to do it my way and in my own time. I was still mad at God. I hadn't even approached the bargaining phase where you promise to help the poor if you are restored to health. Society and medical care could not put that much time into me.

At some point, I was fitted for a pair of prism glasses so I could watch TV while lying flat on my back. This was a major change for me to be able to see something besides floors, feet, and ceiling tiles! I kept those glasses for years. I might still have them. They were green and formed in a block-like triangle so I could view people. They came in their own special brown case. They were dear to me.

3

RANCHO LOS AMIGOS

I HAD BEEN AT HOLY CROSS HOSPITAL for maybe six weeks following my injury when a doctor came in and told me they would be moving me to another hospital very soon. His exact words were, "We have done everything we could for you. The rest is up to you." The rest is up to me? What did that even mean? I was not prepared for this! I had thought that if I was allowed to stay here long enough, I would be able to walk out on my own. Now they were, in effect, telling me that they had done all they could do for me. Now I was being transferred to Ranchos Los Amigos, a rehabilitation hospital in Downey, to learn how to live as a paralyzed man. This was NOT OKAY with me. I needed more time to do it my way. I needed to stay one more month, or maybe two, tops, then I'd be alright. I could go straight to my own home. Somehow I knew that as much as I fought and begged, this doctor knew what was best for me, and he knew that I knew it too. What I didn't know was HOW it would be best for me.

On the morning I was transferred by ambulance to Rancho Los Amigos and assigned to my own room, I made a new friend. Before anyone was assigned to me full-time, he would come in and mop the floors. I never saw his face, only his shoes. He was very kind to me. We would talk, and I would ask him if it was sunny outside, or if it was going to be cloudy or windy. I was high up on the 5th floor where he could see all over the valley. He would always describe to me what he saw.

I was looking up at ceiling tiles again. It was an old building that had treated a lot of patients (including iron lung patients) in the 1950s, before the Salk vaccine kicked in. Oddly, over the years, I had escaped major illnesses even though I wasn't allowed to be inoculated. Ironically, I still ended up paralyzed, just as if I had polio.

Not only couldn't I move, but I felt like I was partially blind, too. I couldn't see anything but ceiling tiles and the floor, and I had to trust other people who knew as little about my care as I did.

There were lots of student nurses in and out during the day; my wife and parents came in the evenings when they could. My parents owned a furniture store and were busy most of the time. My wife was still working as a secretary and trying to handle our bills on her own.

Even though friends and family were constantly in and out of my room—at one time there were 20 in my small room—the hours were endless and the nights sleepless.

My younger brother Jim spent his last year of high school hiding from his friends because he couldn't accept what happened to me. I also think it may have been too painful for him to process the whole situation at his age. Much, much later, in an outburst of anger and frustration, he told me how I had ruined his senior year of high school. He was still angry! Hey, I pretty much ruined my whole year, too! I had been so focused on myself, it had not occurred to me that my friends and family each had their own pain to deal with in relation to my injury and subsequent disabilities. I was still shocked, years later, at the ripple effect my accident had on my family and friends. I had tried to keep everyone's spirits up because I could hear the fear and sadness in their voices as they tried to make small talk. When I was lying on my back, I could see it in their faces.

The days went on and on. Every day I tried to manipulate someone to take me home. I wanted out! I had a clock on the wall. I watched it and thought about things. I thought about how I envied the way people walked; the way they used their hands and fingers to pick things up. If I could, at least, just use my hands! I wanted to feel textures. I dreamt that my hands could feel silk or stone, or the face of a woman. I would be okay with that, I thought. My hands were getting soft and I was becoming ashamed of them. They looked more like the hands of a woman. They used to have calluses, and they were rough. When I worked concrete, even for a day, if I touched my wife's sweater my hands would snag it. I had the hands of a man. Now I had hands like a woman. How could I hope to maintain my grip on life if I didn't, at least, have my hands with which to hold on.

It had been some time since I had seen a mirror. I wasn't excited about seeing my shaved head covered with orange Betadine solution—the new haircut and the thorns in my head—results of the surgery. Yes, there was a mirror in the bathroom at Holy Cross, but of course, I never saw the bathroom. That was used for guests, nurses, and other people who walk. I wondered what I looked like? More powerful was the fear of what I actually did look like, so I avoided the mirror at Holy Cross. A few days after being moved to Rancho Los Amigos, I was taken to the gym and placed right in front of a mirror.

The intention of the aide who put me there was innocent enough, but the effect of seeing myself after all these weeks was traumatic. In a split second, I was stripped of my identity. The person I remembered in my mind's eye was no longer there. I was totally shattered.

After that gut wrenching experience in the gym, I was taken to a ward with five other quadriplegics and left there for five hours, unattended. The smell was overwhelming! I thought for sure I would throw up. We were given showers once a week, and the horrible stench of urine, feces, and body odor told me we were due. It was unbelievable this could be happening. It was more like an asylum you see in horror movies. Quadriplegics and paraplegics have no control over their bowels and bladder; we have to be bathed and changed as needed, just as you would care for a helpless baby. My depression deepened.

We were all spinal injury patients here, so again, I thought they would know how to care for me. Rancho Los Amigos was a teaching hospital where doctors making their rounds, are followed by five or more residents trying to learn as much as they can from the doctors' comments and instruction. When they came to me, the doctor referred to me as a 22-year-old spinal injury with a cervical 3,4 and 5 who would never recover. At best, he will only be able to do telephone sales the rest of his life. Then, they hurriedly moved on to the next patient. He never called me by my name.

Every day, a doctor would come in to check how much external feeling I had in my limbs. He would reach into his pocket and come out with a pin. I think he had it specifically designed to torture quadriplegics—just my opinion. It was a long, silver thing. Sometimes he would use his fountain pen. He would start at my toes and feet, then poke and push and say, "Sharp or dull? Sharp or dull?" Another instrument had little points on the end of a wheel. They roll it down your leg or your arm to determine if you feel anything different from one day to the next. Each day I would plead with God, myself, or my doctors, to let me feel the latest torture device. I used every bit of energy I could muster to move my big toe or to feel a painful jab. When that didn't happen, I hoped that I would experience a little feeling higher in my calf or thigh. One day, I experienced a little feeling in my upper arm, especially my left one. That was as good as it was going to get.

My middle brother Bob delighted in entering the room with an invisible pen and paper saying, "Tell me, sharp or dull? Sharp or dull?" I wasn't amused, but everyone else seemed to be. His ability to make people laugh took the attention off the seriousness in the room.

By Christmas, I was allowed to leave Rancho Los Amigos and go home for a few days. I found myself lying in a lounge chair in the bedroom, looking at ceiling tiles—again. My brothers had to carry me into the house from the truck. Sometimes they would sit me up until I would get dizzy or uncomfortable. You would think that if you were paralyzed you would not feel anything—not true.

There was plenty of pain and discomfort. When I was transferred to Rancho Los Amigos, I was fitted with a catheter and leg bag that collected urine. My catheter was left in place for two long months. It should have been changed and irrigated every two or three days, so my bladder wouldn't become infected. Sometimes, they would clamp on a new catheter and let my bladder fill up to the point where I would become uncomfortable and start sweating. Then, they would clamp it again to teach my bladder to react and empty as much as it could by reflex only. We were all hopeful my bladder might eventually work again. I viewed it as a blessing each time I had a new catheter inserted, and I would feel these chills and goose bumps on my skin.

My bowels didn't have a bag so they had to be trained to evacuate at the same time each day. Often, it was hit and miss. When it missed, I had to be cleaned. When I was on schedule, I had to be lifted on and off the toilet. Sometimes I needed digital stimulation, or suppositories, or a mini enema. It always helped to remain upright, but I had no muscles to support myself. The process could take up to an hour by the time it was completed. I was like a newborn baby. Every function of my body had to be cared for and scrutinized by another person. Some were strangers, some family; others were medical workers or caregivers—both men and women. You lose all sense of privacy, modesty, or decorum.

On the property, there was a lab that made artificial limbs. I remember the smell of the glue and heat mixing together. The people were nice enough to me; but in the end, I considered it was just a job for them to figure out what they could do to help me. I wasn't the best patient. I was given a motorized wheelchair specifically designed for institutional living and instructed to drive myself to the artificial limb lab. You would think I would love the new freedom of movement, but I was scared to death that I would tip over or get stuck and not be able to help myself, even though I knew there were people around to help if I rolled off the grass or walkways. There were big glass doors leading into the buildings that opened automatically. While common in the supermarkets today, they were uncommon at that time. Everything was made easy enough for me to be self-reliant, but humiliation, fear, and failure were waiting around every corner.

I refused help from professionals as well as from people in my similar situation. A man who had become a quadriplegic a few years before me had come to my room to give me a pep talk. I slowly, but firmly, chased him off. Everything he said felt so disconnected and unrelated to me. It occurred to me, seeing him still a quadriplegic after so many years, that I might even be paralyzed for a longer period of time than I had hoped. I was using food (someone had to feed me), sleep (someone had to help me get into position), and television (someone had to turn it on and change the channels) to keep me distracted. A number of perhaps unsavory people also served as a welcome distraction. With a projected lifespan of only 7-12 years, I wasn't motivated to do much for myself.

I looked forward to the weekends and I especially looked forward to Friday when I would beg someone to pick me up and get me out of the rehab hospital. They needed to pick me up in my dad's panel truck—a primitive version of a van—because it accommodated the lounge chair used to transport me. Once home, I found myself staring at yet another set of ceiling tiles. I stared at the ceiling inside my apartment while waiting for my wife to come home from work. I could tell she was totally fatigued. It showed not only in her eyes, but in her whole body. I was selfishly demanding, needing her for everything. I insisted she come to see me at the hospital at least two to three nights a week until she finally became assertive enough to say no. Rancho Los Amigos was almost an hour away from our apartment. Madalena had to drive from Canoga Park, where we lived, to Downey during rush-hour traffic, then drive back home in the evening to get ready for work again the next day. It was taking its toll; but I persisted. I pouted and manipulated, doing my best to make her feel guilty when she didn't come to see me. I was acting like a spoiled child; though in reality, I was terrified. I was terrified at how dependent I was on her and the rest of my family. I needed them to come and get me out of the hospital, if only for the weekend. What if they were too busy to make the trip, or too exhausted to take care of me, or worse, didn't want to? And how I dreaded going back on Sunday evenings. By late Sunday afternoon, I was sliding back into my shell and becoming pouty again.

I wanted no part of the hour long drive back to the facility. I also didn't want to learn how to feed myself. They tried to teach me by strapping a spoon onto my arm. The bowl of the spoon swiveled as I inched my arm toward my mouth. As soon as it got close, the spoon swiveled again and the food dropped out—onto me, the floor, everywhere but into my mouth. I told the aide I would rather make a lot of money and hire someone to feed me! I didn't want to learn how to write. I didn't want to learn how to dress myself. I wanted none of it! The reality was that I couldn't do much of anything, no matter how they tried to teach me. I just didn't have enough moving parts.

No one knew how to deal with a "quad" in 1965. Our projected life span was substantially less than 12 years. We usually died of lung or kidney failure. Paraplegics who had sustained spinal cord injuries in WWII were barely surviving. There was some minimal success with paraplegics, but for the most part they were written off. There was no help, no ability to save them.

After many long months at Rancho Los Amigos, I pretty much understood my physical status; it broke my heart over and over again. I had seen other patients gather strength and regain use of some parts of their bodies. I thought I could will my hands to work again! If I could just feed myself, or dress myself, or push my own chair. At least I would be more self-sufficient like them. But it wasn't to be.

I spoke to a woman who was very connected to the spiritual part of ourselves. I told her my parents were praying for me; they had churches praying for me; they hired a practitioner to pray for me, and I believed in this. I said, "I can't understand why I …" She interrupted me saying, "It is working to the level you allow it to work!" What?!!!

The nuts and bolts of the next part of my life were the "what if," the "only if," the "why not," and the "why me." I hated to be selfish and boring, but growth takes time! And I had a lot more growing to do. I was angry for years, almost six years to be exact, and not entirely wrongfully so because of the negligence, poor care, and actual damage done to me in the hospitals.

4

COMING HOME

BY AUGUST OF 1966, I said goodbye to Rancho Los Amigos for the last time. My brother Bob helped my wife and me find a nice little house for $125 per month in Canoga Park. There I stayed while Madalena went off to work each day. I was fairly isolated since I wanted little or nothing to do with the neighbors. We lived in the little house a couple of years until Madalena threw in the towel. Madalena was completely overwhelmed and getting sick from all the pressure that she was ill-equipped and unprepared to handle. She was seeing a psychiatrist to help her find her way through our situation. I was not helping. She told me she would stay with me forever if I would just try, but I was so angry, I couldn't. We agreed it was time for her to move on.

After the divorce, I moved back in with my parents on Petit Street in Northridge where I was raised. They didn't go out of their way to make any accommodations for me, such as moving furniture to make my access—ingress and egress—less difficult. I don't know if this was tough love or it just never occurred to them how impossible it was for me to be maneuvered around the furniture without bumping into it. I did bump into stuff all the time. No one said a word.

In spite of that, my mother was my friend and helper. She would get up in the middle of the night to turn me over if I felt stuck. Sometimes, the pillow would get too close to my face and

I couldn't move it away. She was the one who gave me a book by Norman Vincent Peale, *The Power of Positive Thinking*. It planted a seed.

I remember one day when I was whining about not being able to do anything in my wheelchair. My mother, whether out of anger or frustration, or both, said, "Quit complaining. If you really wanted to get out of that wheelchair, you'd do it." WHAT? Not again? Do they all think like that?! With every bit of rage that I had bottled up, I screamed, and I kicked, and I tried to move all of my muscles—to no avail. Talk about angry! Words cannot describe the level of my rage and the betrayal I felt from my own mother. Every day, I tried to will my hands and feet to move with every force inside me. I tried to move my head to the side, even just the tiniest little bit. It took me years to forgive my mother. We had been so close; I felt totally betrayed by her words. Anger can have a very long curve.

For years after that, I beat myself up and second-guessed myself. Could I have worked harder, could I have done more? How sad to raise a child that way; a child who must ultimately fail God, his family, and lose all respect for himself in the bargain.

In spite of the setbacks, I found myself once again living in my old neighborhood, this time, noticing how nice it was; it was a real community. As I braved sitting outside and being exposed for everyone to see, I realized how tremendously supportive and concerned other people were toward me. Some were nosey, some liked to gossip, but all and all, when push came to shove, they were there for each of us in a sense of community. On a long Saturday or Sunday, when no one was home at my house, it felt good to know there would be someone who would give me a few moments of kindness and consideration.

> *"Love Your Crooked Neighbor*
> *With All Your Crooked Heart."*
>
> – W.H. Auden

I love to sit in the sun. When I am wheeled outside in my manual chair, I cannot move myself at all. When I first moved back to my parents' house, I enlisted someone—my brothers, neighbors, or a hired person—to take me outdoors. Then I told them to leave. I wanted to be by myself and not have them hanging around trying to make small talk. I didn't care if I got sunburned. I didn't care if I died. I was doomed anyway, so I tempted fate all the time. I just sat in the sun, either in my wheelchair or in the pool on a floating chair, until someone came by to take me inside and feed me or give me water. I punished myself. It was brutal.

I had helpers put me in the floating device in the pool. One time a neighbor kid who helped me into the pool and he was supposed to come back in a couple of hours to retrieve me. When he didn't appear, I started yelling toward the fence for him to come over. When he didn't respond, I yelled louder and longer. My neighbor got tired of hearing all the racket and shouted back over the fence, "Will you shut up, already?" I yelled back at him, "Come over here and make me!" At this, he jumped up to look over the fence, saw me, and said, "Oh, shit." But he didn't come to help me, either. By the time my family arrived home, I was sunburned, thirsty, hungry, and no longer having fun.

The prospect of living like this for years and then dying anyway did not fill me with joy. I would gladly have taken my life at any time if I could have. I prayed to God to die, but God had other plans for me. I was told:

"God Answers Your Prayers in Three Different Ways:
Yes
Not Yet
I Have Something Better in Mind."

– Anonymous

It would still be years before I knew what He had in mind.

Sitting in the sun for a quadriplegic is similar to being in the sun for people who have been burned in a fire. When your skin is severely burned, the pores are destroyed and your skin cannot breathe. Your skin cannot sweat. Your body retains it. The same things happen to paraplegics and quadriplegics, especially when their body thermostat has shut down. The intensity of your inner heat becomes so great it feels as if you are sitting in a pressure cooker. Although we can stay out in the sun for a while, heat frustration can build up immediately.

Besides dealing with the sun, I had to contend with getting too close to fires and flames, guessing when it was too hot, as when sitting next to the fireplace. My skin could be almost blistered and I wouldn't feel the heat. On one occasion, I got second degree burns on my fingers because I wanted to hold a cigar between my index and middle fingers. I had a rubber band wrapped around the cigar to hold it in place while I sat outside smoking. I smelled an odd burning odor and finally realized it was my own flesh! Another time, I sat too long next to a fire place. The next morning, I woke up with blisters on my hands and legs. Sometimes, I even got blisters on the inside of my hand from holding a coffee cup! Like I said before, I had that hard learning curve! I was constantly being reminded that I could not feel things the way I could before the accident.

"I Want to Tell You It Gets Better.
It Doesn't Get Better. You Get Better."

– Joan Rivers

5

OBSERVING DETERMINATION

Two years after the accident, my friends and relatives still came to visit me. Sometimes I welcomed them, and sometimes I wanted nothing to do with them. At first, I was glad my friends, work mates, and classmates came to visit. My mother Marge was very social and loved cooking for visitors. Jerry Larson came to visit often. Jerry was my best friend from high school. He was in an accident and lost an arm in a meat grinder when he was 17. Over the years we would joke and tell people we have been friends for so long that I remember when Jerry had an arm and I could walk! Jerry kept in touch through the years and was very influential in how my life would eventually play out.

When I ventured outside in my chair, I noticed how some parents were quite uncomfortable around me. Not the kids, their parents. The neighborhood kids would come up to me and ask me questions like, "What happened to you?" or "How do you brush your teeth?" I loved their candidness, and I wanted to answer their questions and tell them how we were different and how we were the same. Parents would rush up and tell the children to, "Leave the man alone." or "Don't bother the man." When I told them it was okay, I didn't mind, they would say something like, "We don't want to confuse the children," and pulled them away.

"Everything Will Be Okay in the End.
If It's Not Okay, It's Not the End."

– John Lennon

Eventually, I would learn two important life lessons from those encounters: 1. That I was the one who projected ignorance and rejection in my own attitude about my disability, and 2. That there was a gift inside of each one of us. Even though the package may be damaged, that gift inside us could make a difference. It could give a purpose to a life. We need to be open and let those people who care about us nurture that gift out of us—love it out of us.

From my chair, most of all, I enjoyed watching and observing the youngest ones who visited.

I was fascinated by the tenacity of my nine-month-old niece who kept trying and trying to grab something off of the coffee table she wasn't supposed to have. No matter what the reprimand, it wasn't good enough for her. I was told a similar story about my sister-in-law who, as a baby, was told not to grab an ash tray, that it wasn't for children. After several attempts, where she was repelled by her mother saying, "If you reach for that one more time, I am going to slap your hand." She tried again. In defiance, she looked her mother straight in the eye, took the ash tray, tucked it under her arm, and laid out her hand to be slapped. She knew the consequences, but the accomplishment was so much more powerful than the punishment.

"Anger and Stubbornness Are Best Friends,
They Need Each Other For Fuel."

– Jackson Tavini

Where does that determination go? Did I ever have that kind of tenacity, or did it leave me when I had my accident? Having given it much thought since then, I do believe we all have it in us. It may not always be evident, but the power is still there when we need it. We are told not to take risks, to remain commonplace, and then, when we do not succeed, we are reminded, "I told you so!" The words, "I told you so," are the greatest shame reinforcement for inducing discouragement that I have ever heard.

As time rolled on, however, I began to tire of seeing the children progress as I remained the same. I also tired of hearing how my friends were traveling, or going water skiing, or even living on the third floor of a nice apartment building, while I was still in my chair going nowhere. I started to compare my life to theirs and found it lacking in almost every way. I didn't have anything to look forward to except certain death in a shorter period of time than most.

I didn't want to watch Playboy television or subscribe to *Playboy* because all it did was remind me of everything I could no longer do. I was locked into the belief that I could never have another relationship again. I was done. I was feeling the panic of falling behind all of my friends. I was approaching 30 and had nothing to show for my life. I was living at home with Mom and Dad and running out of my small stipend of government money by the first or second week of the month. I had to take from them and rely on them for food and shelter. I had no car to go anywhere—even if I could talk someone into taking me.

I reached a point when I realized that I had to stop comparing myself to my friends, if only to sustain my own sanity. Maybe we weren't in the same competitive race, or even using the same standards. I tried to think what I would be like in their shoes. What kind of a person would I have to become to be successful—one who is willing to hurt, manipulate, cheat, or step on others to reach my goals? Some of my friends bragged about the illegal means they used to get what they wanted. Sometimes, I didn't like myself because I thought their behaviors were okay. At least they made it. I didn't.

"Make the Present Moment Your Friend,
Not Your Enemy."

– Unknown

People told me all the time that I could do more. I could be powerful and successful in anything I put my mind to. Maybe I could be a teacher. Since I like to argue so much, maybe I would do well in law or I like to think about things and I am interested in people, so maybe I would do well in psychology.

What a joke. I was average in the brains department. In high school, there were "jocks" and there were the "A" students who I referred to as the "Fauntleroys." They were the kids who got the scholarships. How could I identify with the smart kids? I thought psychologists were weird; telling your problems to some stranger made you even weaker than you were! At that time, I didn't understand the benefit of taking the risk of revealing yourself to someone else in order to learn more about *yourself*, and not so much for what the other the other person might say to you.

I thought a lot. In the evenings sitting alone, in spite of my anger, in spite of the fact that I didn't care what happened to me, I would pose theoretical questions to myself. What if there was a fire? What would I do? What if I couldn't get myself out? What if...? I could feel the panic welling up inside of me and bringing tears to my eyes. The frozen kind of tears that go unexpressed. Nothing. I could do nothing. For the five or six years after my accident, and before I made the decision to go back to school, I was all about distracting myself from myself. I was very, very depressed.

6

SICK AND TIRED OF BEING SICK AND TIRED

WHEN I STARTED CONSIDERING the possibility that my life could be different, I could focus my attention on something more valuable than constant misery. Maybe I could get interested in something else. So this notion of creating a different life mentally through my thoughts started to kick in.

> *"No Matter How Many Mistakes You Make*
> *or How Slow Your Progress,*
> *You Are Still Way Ahead of Everyone Who Isn't Trying."*
>
> - Tony Robbins

I began to read. As I began reading for longer periods of time, parts of my body became fatigued. Pain and eye strain developed from looking down, telling me, "It's time to stop now, it's time to quit and go lie down." The other part of me was saying, "No, just a little bit longer." I could feel my body starting to sweat, telling me to get out of that chair or at least change position. I needed help to move, but there were rarely people around me anymore. I had pushed them away.

So I pushed myself. I sat a little bit longer each time, worked a bit longer, read a bit longer, and asked people to help me more often. Although frustrating everyone around me by my needs, I began making steady progress. Tenacity was alive and well!

There was something building inside of me. Maybe it was anger. Maybe it was that moment when you feel you are going to get tough and stop punishing yourself. So I continued on. I continued to sit, I continued to read, I continued to hang in there. Even when others would say, "It's time to stop now. Aren't you done yet?" I became more obsessive and compulsive about what I was doing. I had never met anyone as obsessive nor as compulsive as I eventually would become. Now, I was driving people away from me for a different reason. I was wearing them out! I wouldn't stop, nor could I stop. Now I was accused of overcompensating! I was trying to improve myself, or prove myself, and in doing so, exhausting everyone else. Maybe all this introspection has served to make me more aware of how sick and tired I was of being sick and tired. I needed to make a shift in how I saw things.

I didn't even realize how strong this drive had become. I just knew that by DOING something, I could distract myself from the ever-present pain and hopelessness.

For years I fed off of anger and resentment. Most of my friends had backed away. I am what I call a "hard learner"—or a hard head. Maybe there is no difference. But I was alone more often than not. My fault.

Now I was determined to focus only on what I COULD do. None who knew me thought I should, or even could, go back to school. In my walking years, I flunked out of junior college. I was an average student and an average guy. Actually, maybe not so average, since I did flunk out. I preferred playing pool, drinking beer, and having fun to attending classes and doing homework. Changes were needed. I had to make up all the classes I failed before I would be accepted as a permanent student.

It wasn't easy. None of it was ever easy. Had I listened to my doctor at Rancho Los Amigos, I might have ended up being a telephone sales caller as he predicted!

7

BACK TO SCHOOL

IT WAS AROUND 1970 when I started back to school at Pierce Community College to make up my previously failed classes. That done, I transferred to California State University at Northridge. I still could not sit for much longer than 45 minutes at a time. I had an attendant wheel me around to my classes, take notes, assist me with bathroom chores, and feed me. In between classes, he would wheel me out to the parking lot to my van, open the door, and help me stretch out over a big pile of pillows so I could ease the un-remitting, ever present pain for 30 to 45 minutes. He would then leave for a break and come back later to take me to the next class. Thank God for California's sunny days so I could do what I needed to do to continue on.

In the early 70s, there were no amenities for the handicapped. There were no ramps, no automatic doors, no cut-outs in the curb for wheelchairs. Even if I had an electric chair, which I didn't, it wouldn't have been helpful. A lot of the classes were on the second floor. It was scary asking people to carry me up the stairs in my chair. I couldn't bear the thought of falling again if my helpers dropped me. The chair was part of me now. If it didn't go, I didn't go. At least a manual chair didn't weigh as much as the electric ones did; some of those weighed in at 350 pounds. In class, I either had to ask willing students to share their notes with me so I could use them to study, or I had to hire someone to come to my classes and take notes.

"I Have No Special Talents, I Am Only Passionately Curious."

- Albert Einstein

I was alone during the day when I studied at home, so I had to learn to turn pages with my knuckle. I had always had some movement in my left shoulder, which made that possible—but problematic. I was right-handed and learning to use my left arm. Every once in a while, I would bump my book and knock it to the floor, where it stayed for hours until my parents came home to retrieve it for me. I can't emphasize enough how very dependent I was on others for everything.

My tests were all verbal by necessity, so I eventually turned to the National Speakers Association to improve my communication skills. It seems there was always another roadblock to overcome!

Someone once said, "Never say never." It almost draws you to that experience which you are trying to avoid. It seems like you take an extra quantum leap towards that end. I never wanted to become someone involved in the area of mental health. Probably because I was afraid that my own mental health was in such disarray, I didn't think I could help anyone else. So, of course, I became a psychology major.

Dr. Irving Bloom was my psychology professor. He was located in Santa Barbara at the Fielding Institute where I had to go to complete my doctorate. His classes were held on the second floor. I asked Dr. Bloom if he would teach me, one on one, at his ground- floor office in the institute since it was so difficult for me to get to the second floor for his class—let alone have someone drive me to Santa Barbara. And there were no elevators in his building! I required some pretty strong and willing young men to carry me upstairs in my chair. Dr. Bloom explained that I was no different than any other student and would be expected to show up for class like everyone else. This was news to me! It never occurred to me that I wasn't different from everyone else. Another lesson learned from the good doctor: The world didn't revolve around David Van Gorder. I was, unbeknownst to me, finally learning what it meant to be a "real man." Darn! I loved Dr. Bloom and he loved me. We remained friends for many years.

My friend Jerry Larson, whom I mentioned earlier, was a big influence on me in every way. He kept me going when life would get tough. Jerry was such a good friend that I could call him when I needed an ego boost. "Jerry," I would say, "Tell me I am a good person. Tell me you care about me." He would tell me, "Dave, you are a good person and I care about you." And I would do the same for him. Sometimes you just need a reminder.

As a psychology major, I was required to undergo therapy. I was very much opposed to the idea, as I was secretly afraid that I was probably mentally ill by this time and possibly beyond redemption. After my last year and last round of intense therapy, Dr. Bloom told me, "David, you can't have your ass in two saddles." I couldn't ride two horses at the same time. It was time to take a stand and stop sitting on the fence. I had to be more positive. All in all, it wasn't as bad as I thought it would be, which was a huge relief.

My dissertation was the last straw. I was ready to walk—or roll—away. My paper was so long that the committee kept refusing it! I was compulsive; they were adamant. After much angst on both our parts, the committee finally accepted my reduced version of the *Encyclopedia Britannica*. I was so disgusted by then that I didn't even attend graduation.

It took 16 dogged years to complete my doctorate program in psychology and earn my Psy.D. degree. If you are keeping track, I was probably forty or forty-four years-old. I had my master's degree, so I was already teaching and getting in my required hours. I was the dreaded mind doctor! It seemed as if everything I knew I didn't want to do, I was bound to do. This was also partly Jerry's influence, as he had become a psychologist many years ahead of me. His daughter Chamile followed in our footsteps many years after that. I guess she thought we were having too much fun.

The Fielding Institute

Upon recommendation of the Faculty and by the
authority of the Board of Trustees, hereby confers upon

David A. Van Gorder

the degree of

Doctor of Psychology

with an emphasis in Clinical Psychology

with all honors, rights and privileges thereto appertaining.

In testimony whereof the undersigned have subscribed their names and affixed the seal
of the Institute at Santa Barbara, California on this day,

the eighteenth day of September, nineteen hundred and eighty-seven.

_____
Chair, Board of Trustees

_____
Program Chair

_____
William H. Machl
President

_____
Marvin M. Bloom
For the Faculty

THE FIELDING INSTITUTE
1974

Ordinary People Do Extraordinary Things

During this entire time, I was raking in the hefty sum of $71.40 twice a month from the government as a disability payment. I couldn't support myself on that amount of money, so I was totally dependent on my parents for help. I still lived with them on Petit Street in my childhood home. Since I was given only 7-12 years to live, I think the insurance company was holding out as long as they could to offer any real compensation. My original insurance company, through my construction job, had gone out of business and another company bought out the claims.

I met a lawyer when I was in college, and he encouraged me to settle for $600,000. I didn't think that would cover my needs for a lifetime, and I refused. Actually, I never settled. If I had, I could never petition for more if and when I needed it, and I always needed more.

8

NATIONAL SPEAKERS ASSOCIATION

As I MENTIONED, I became a member of the National Speakers Association (similar to Toastmasters) during the years I was in college. As in everything I did, I was compulsive about it. Plus, I found I really enjoyed speaking. I could talk, and I could argue, and I was learning to read with an eye for making my cases.

I was eventually honored with the highest award they bestow: The Council of Peers Award of Excellence. In my acceptance speech, I spoke to my friends, acknowledging how often we forget to thank our friends or to recognize those who have contributed to our success. I said, "Can you think back 20 years and see how much you have accomplished in that time? How much you have learned? How much you have done? How many people you have touched in the last 20 years? The difference that you have made? Think about how far you have come; then think about how much further you can go. Then think about the difference you are going to make in the next day, the next week, and the next year." I meant every word.

I read a lot of biographies for personal encouragement along the way. Among the most outstanding, and indeed memorable, was that of W. Mitchell, whom I came to know personally as my friend. He is also a recipient of the Council of Peers Award of Excellence. W. Mitchell began a radio career in Hawaii, as a member of the US Marine Corps. He drove cable cars in San

Francisco, then went on to found a metal castings company that employed thousands of people in the North East. As a civic leader of Crested Butte, Colorado, he gained international recognition as "The Mayor who saved the mountain." He is a pilot and a white-water rafter. In his 1984 campaign for Congress, his campaign slogan was, "Oh yes I can." His message to us all was, "It's not what happens to you, it's what you do about it."

W. Mitchell was true to his word. He accomplished most of these things after two catastrophic accidents that left him disfigured and in a wheel chair. At the time of his first injury, he was burned when a laundry truck turned in front of the motorcycle he was riding in San Francisco. His face was gone, his hands were badly scarred and his fingers badly burned. He lost most of each of his 10 fingers and very nearly his life. He had just completed his first solo aircraft flight before his accident. After his burns healed, he went on to complete his pilot training.

On November 22, 1975, while on a business trip for Vermont Castings, he injured his spinal cord in an airplane crash while piloting his own plane. As a result, he became paralyzed from the waist down. He could have succumbed to the "life is not fair" philosophy and would not have been faulted. Instead, he chose to demonstrate the invincibility of the human spirit. In 1977, he ran for and was elected mayor of Crested Butte, Colorado.

W. Mitchell has told his story around the world hundreds of times. You might have read it in a magazine or heard it on Paul Harvey's "The Rest of the Story" radio program.

"Start by Doing What is Necessary; Then Do What Is Possible; And Suddenly You Are Doing the Impossible."

\- Unknown

W. Mitchell gave me hope and kept me going when I needed it. I am very grateful for his inspiration.

Besides W. Mitchell's own story, I was inspired by another true story that I heard at one of our National Speakers Association meetings. Here is that story.

A dentist was driving home one night with his fiancé and hit a gasoline truck. He was burned beyond his own recognition, and his fiancé was killed immediately. After months and months of touch and go on an hourly basis, the doctors finally told his family that he would probably live. His family asked, "Live for what?" When the dentist had his tragic accident, he was on his way home to get ready to compete in the Iron Man Marathon, for which he had trained many years. For those of you who haven't heard of the Iron Man challenge, it takes place in Hawaii where contestants must swim 4.2 miles in the ocean, ride their bikes over a prescribed course of 112 miles, then run for 26 miles! Impossible undertaking for most of us.

Back to the hospital. The dentist had been burned almost the entire length of his body. He wasn't expected to walk again. Because he had sustained so much damage in the fire, his legs couldn't hold the weight of his own body. He did eventually stand, much to the surprise of his doctor. Several months out of the hospital, his mother came around to his house and found him practicing his iron man techniques. His mother, totally alarmed, called the doctor and said, "Tell him to stop. It's going to hurt him. It's not good for him." The doctor told her, "It's alright; I talked to him about this. At least he has a dream. At least he has a goal. At least he has some kind of focus. Leave him alone. It's impossible, yeah, but don't discourage him. Do not discourage him."

The dentist, way in the back of the crowd, was in an Iron Man suit with a number on his burned arm. His family was with him cheering loudly. They shouted, "You have done more to get to the starting line than anyone would have done who got to the finish line! You don't even have to start running. You could just walk along with the crowd, watching the rest of the race. He responded, "I just want to go a little bit farther. I just want to see what I can do!" About a quarter mile into the race, the family said, "OK, that's good now. Quit now, that's it." The dentist yelled over his shoulder, "Stop it. I just want to go a little farther."

I thought to myself, it helps to have the belief and confidence in your ability already in place when tragedy strikes. It is more challenging never to have felt true confidence. Knowing you have accomplished this one little thing, you might now be able to do this next overwhelming, insurmountable task. For many of us, that notion is just not there. We must imagine the possibility that, at some level, confidence exists within us. We must discover it, and refine it, and use it. That is exactly what I had to do.

9

PRACTICING THERAPIST

THERE I WAS at the age of forty-three, sixteen plus years after I began my college experience, I had earned my Psy.D degree and I was still living with my parents. My dad and my brother fixed up the garage to be my new office. It was quite nice with wood paneling and all. In those days, I was learning, challenging myself, and always wanting to learn more. It was my first real opportunity to feel purposeful. I was enthusiastic!

I worked with individual clients in my garage office at the house. Jerry was instrumental in getting me a position five days a week at California State University Dominguez Hills, where I taught classes for alcohol and drug abuse for the next 10 years. Every day, I had to be driven from Northridge to Dominquez Hills, not returning home until 11 p.m. on most nights. I relied on a lot of people to accomplish that, and I appreciated each and every one of them.

My not having alcohol as a drug of choice seemed to irritate my students. They would just look at me and say, "Well, you're not an alcoholic or drug addict. You don't understand." I'd say, "Do you have to fall off a roof and break your neck to come sit before me and empathize that I'm hurting? I don't recommend that you fall off a roof, break your neck, or go through divorces, self-shame, and negative relationships to be able to turn your life around. You come to this place to be able to see things differently."

"The Two Most Important Days in Your Life
Are the Day You Are Born
and the Day You Find Out Why."

- Mark Twain

To be successful, you don't have to wind up in a wheelchair, or recover from alcohol, or some other problems. You just don't have to do that! You can learn from other people. You can read biographies, the Bible, watch videos, or talk to people. You will find these are not remarkable people, but they have done remarkable things. They have taken risks to move ahead, and they have met challenges.

I was a great believer in disseminating information, and I kept the Xerox machines busy until most everyone else had left for the evening. I had been at Dominguez Hills for 10 years when I got another a call from Jerry.

Jerry was now running the show at Pasadena Community Hospital. He hired me to work there with women addicted to drugs and/or alcohol and women with mental issues.

David teaching nurses at Yavapai College.

10

MEETING MARY

PASADENA COMMUNITY HOSPITAL is where my life changed in leaps and bounds for the better—I met my future wife Mary. I will let her tell you our story. We became friends when she was hired on as a temporary nurse, and we became closer and closer as they extended her temporary status.

When Pasadena Community Hospital lost funding, Mary and I moved on to Pine Grove Psychiatric Hospital in Encino. We have worked together ever since. She became my office manager and right-hand "man"! As our relationship progressed, Mary and I bought a little house together in Northridge, California. My mother had passed on March 27, 1986. I wanted to live on the same street as my dad and my brother Bob. I told Mary I would give her two years; then, she would probably leave me so I wanted to be close to my family when I needed help. You can tell I wasn't very trusting, and certainly not what you would call a romantic.

*"For Once in My Life,
I Have Someone Who Loves Me."*
- Ronald Miller & Orlando Murden

We did find a house across the street from Bob and down the block from my dad. It was in pretty sorry shape and needed some remodeling—well, a lot of remodeling. We paid top dollar for it, primarily for the location. Then we got busy and had the remodeling crew come in. It didn't have air conditioning! This was the valley. It was HOT in the summer. We moved into the garage and set up camp where we could cook while the workers busied themselves making our new home into a proper house. During the summer, we put netting over the garage door so we could keep the door open and the bugs out.

"I Have Failed Over and Over and Over Again in My Life,
And That Is Why I Succeeded."

- Michael Jordan

New house on Calahan Street, Northridge, CA.

11

NEW HOUSE

I WOULD GO TO MY DAD'S HOUSE to meet with patients in my garage office. Dad had converted my old bedroom into another office for me where Mary took care of the administrative details. Mary was back and forth from my father's house to our house throughout the day—cooking, errands, and whatever she had to do. When Mary was too busy or unavailable to pick me up, I drove myself home in the electric chair, barreling down the street in the dark. Mary was afraid I would run into something and hurt myself since there were no curbs or sidewalks so she arranged to have someone put lights on my wheelchair. That worked as long as someone remembered to turn them on for me.

Every day, I made it a point to go to the park and have a therapy session with Mary. I knew how stressed she was with workers in the house six days a week. Her long divorce was also finally reaching its end. The park gave us time to be together in a peaceful setting. It was wonderfully relaxing. At night, we could retire to the bedroom in the new house, the only room that was currently livable.

"Everything You've Ever Wanted Was on The
Other Side of Fear."

- George Addair

All this time, Mary had taken on the responsibility of getting me in and out of bed. She had to move my chair next to the bed, put my legs on the bed, and hook a strap around me to pull me out of the chair and onto the bed. There was a lot of pushing and pulling until I was on the bed. I couldn't help her. I was dead weight. Then Mary repositioned the strap and stood over me, legs straddling on each side of me and "dead lifted" me two or three times until she could get me in position. Then began the rolling to the left and to the right so she could undress me and get me into bed—then hook up the night jug (for urine). That was the first time her back went out, and she had to have surgery. It was obvious to everyone we needed help.

We were very fortunate to find an attorney in Encino, named Barry Cohen. We liked each other right away, and he took the insurance company to court for the first of many times. He was a fighter, and he fought for us. Barry was appalled that the insurance company would refuse to pay for attendants, and that Mary had to have back surgery from trying to lift me! Barry terrorized the insurance company, or at the least, wrote persuasive letters. Over the years, Barry would take the insurance company to court many times to get a new wheelchair; or a van; or more money for aides, surgery and physical therapy, a pace maker, more tests, exercise equipment, and more doctors' visits. The insurance company was so ornery and evasive at being forced to pay punitive damages more than once. There was no end to it. Eventually, instead of a file with the insurance company, I had accumulated an entire shelf!

Barry never charged us a dime. He joked that he was making about $1.25 an hour off of us, but he never sent us a bill. The only compensation he ever got was taking a small part of the punitive damages that were awarded against the insurance company. He was a Godsend. I needed more things as I got older. Mary, physically, did a lot of the work it took to care for me, or we would have spent a fortune on 24/7 care. She called it her contribution, since she could no longer work outside of the home.

Remodeling construction finally ceased. The house was finished! And it was beautiful. Mary and I were so very pleased to have a home of our own, and a handicapped accessible one to boot. Wide hallways meant no more running into furniture, finally!

The year was 1991. This was the first time since 1967 that I had lived out of my parents' house.

12

RV

WITH EVERYTHING UNDER CONTROL on the home front, I wanted to buy an RV so we could travel for business and for pleasure. I would have everything I needed with me all the time. We ordered a nice RV that suited our needs, then proceeded to tear it apart and refit it. We equipped it with a lift to help get me in and out of bed. Mary still had to fit me into the harness and attach it to a pully that was installed in the ceiling. She would pump a lever up and down, much like pumping a water pump, and the lift would pull me up where I could be dressed or undressed as the case may be, or swung up onto the bed. I used the chair to get into the shower seat in the roll-in shower. We had a bus lift installed so I could get into the RV. Extra wide doors opened from the middle, outward to each side. A big lift extended down to the ground where I could roll the chair onto it. Mary pushed a lever to pop up a latch, thereby holding the chair in place.

"If You're Always Trying to Be Normal
You Will Never Know How Amazing You Can Be."

- Maya Angelo

Then I discovered the RV store! Like a kid in a candy shop, I couldn't help myself. We bought outside lights, chairs, games, gold mining pans (yes, gold mining pans). I ordered things I thought Mary might like. I wanted a tall ice bucket to keep my beer cold while we sat outside in the evening. Chips, beer, and a cowboy hat. I was set. If it killed Mary, we were going to have fun!

We did have fun. On a memorable trip to Northern California, we stopped at a Placerville campground situated on a cliff overlooking the American River. I very much wanted Mary to have a good time, so I arranged for her to have gold panning lessons—I knew those gold mining pans would come in handy! I sat in the campground overlooking the river so I could watch Mary while an old miner taught her how to swish the water in the pan. She started to throw the water back into the river. The miner yelled, "Wait! I see something." He took the pan from her and secretly dropped a gold nugget into it as we had previously planned. I had paid the old guy $50 to make sure she found gold.

"I found Gold! I found gold! I found a gold nugget!" Mary was dancing and yelling and running up the hill to show me her gold. "David, I found gold!" She was so excited, I just couldn't tell her it was planted. I just let her enjoy the moment. However, the moment got out of hand when she wanted to pan for gold every day; and the next year, she brought her mother back with us to find gold. Her mother fell into the river searching for gold. I didn't tell her the truth for years; I was in it too deep by then. When Mary finally did find out, she was furious. She felt she had made a fool of herself and got her mom dunked in the river to boot. She threatened, not for the first time, to tip me out of my chair when I misbehaved!

Back in Northridge, when our house was finished and we were officially moved in, Mary and I went shopping for an engagement ring. She has always remembered that I did not actually ask her to marry me, I just gave her a ring. Still not romantic, but it also didn't give her the opportunity to say no. I think it is called an "assumptive close." It worked and we set a date.

Mary worked very hard, as she always did, and created a beautiful, comfortable home and a glorious yard full of flowers.

"Forever and Ever, Amen."

—Paul Overstreet & Don Schlitz

13

THE WEDDING

WE WERE MARRIED in the back yard surrounded by friends
and family on September 28, 1991. My dad and brothers came.
My mother had passed away by then. Neighbors we had known
for years showed up. Mary's father had also passed away, but
her mother Lena, and sister Sue and brother-in-law Tom were
there. Mary's son Shawn gave her away, and her daughter Angela
was her maid of honor. Other cousins had made long journeys
to attend as well. My best friend Jerry was my best man. There
were wait staff walking around the yard serving guests catered
appetizers, and there was an open bar for everyone. Tables with
elegant black table cloths dotted the lawn. It was September. I
thought it would be cooler than it turned out to be, so I had
ordered a heavy winter-weight tux. I had to escape inside for a
few minutes throughout the festivities in order to cool down. It
was 107 degrees!

I rented a grand piano to be delivered and set outside on
the lawn. Karen Rae, a good friend, offered to play. I was fairly
musical. Remember the accordion? I had a pretty good voice,
so I picked three songs I wanted to sing for Mary. I hoped I
could get my brothers to sing background with me on the last
one, "Evergreen". They were like a box of cats. No help at all. I
sang my songs and we were pronounced married. I wanted to
take Mary's garter off, but I couldn't bend my neck, so one of the

guests picked her up and held her leg in front of me, allowing me to pull off her garter with my teeth. I thought Mary would die of embarrassment. Jerry helped me throw it into the crowd.

When it came time to cut the cake, I reminded Mary to be careful feeding me the cake, as I was handicapped. She should have seen that coming, because she was always dainty and careful. Now it was my turn to feed her. She put a piece of cake on the back of my hand and I smeared it onto her face. I claimed I had a spasm, but the mischievous look on my face gave me away. Later in the evening, I thought it would be fun to have more singing, so I opened up the garage for karaoke. Thus ended a fun, happy wedding.

"TODAY I MARRIED MY BEST FRIEND."

Backyard Wedding - September 28, 1991

14

THE HONEYMOON

TEN DAYS AND TWO ATTENDANTS LATER, we flew to Hawaii for our honeymoon after the last of our guests headed home.

Traveling is always an adventure. Many have called me brave for putting my life in the hands of people who may or may not know what they are doing. I always say, "What could happen? I'll fall and break my neck?" And so, we were off to the Islands. The first thing we had to do to prepare for our trip was to build a substantial box in which to ship my wheelchair. It was huge and heavy. Then we had it trucked to Los Angeles International Airport.

People with special issues had to arrive at the airport 2-3 hours ahead of their flight. Airline personnel transferred me into a manual chair with no padding or cushion. You might think this doesn't matter—that people with spinal injuries have no feeling, but we do. I feel my insides, not my skin. I have ever present and painful arthritis from the accident; and there are many other problems that can occur once you have a catastrophic injury. At that moment, however, all I could think of was my custom-made electric wheelchair. It weighs 350 pounds! The weight catches cargo loaders by surprise. On a previous trip to Washington D.C. the loaders dropped it off of the conveyer belt and it ultimately had to be replaced. The $30,000 replacement cost required another letter from Barry Cohen, and it took months to finally get a new chair. Thus, the purpose of the box.

I wear a corset to hold me sitting up straight. It slides up and out of place each time I am lifted in or out of my chair. It is uncomfortable under ideal circumstances. Out of place it exerts a lot of pressure on my lungs. Once on a plane, they begin the effort of lifting me over the arm of the aisle seat. The arm does not lift up to make it easy, so two or three men have to get me into position without hurting me or themselves. By this time, I am sweating. Stress does that. I am always the first one seated, and I am placed in the first-row aisle seat. As the rest of the passengers enter the cabin, I am hit with a barrage of luggage, knapsacks, diaper bags, purses, and assorted laptops. I cannot "duck and weave" or move my head at all as they might expect me to do—if they even thought about it at all.

When we arrived in Honolulu, it was the same process repeated in reverse. We wait for my chair to be off loaded; then we wait for a handicapped van to become available. I cannot bend my neck to tip my head down in order to fit into a normal height van. I only fly non-stop for all of the above reasons! All in all, it was worth it for a fun and memorable honeymoon.

15

THE EARTHQUAKE

LESS THAN THREE YEARS after we bought our house in Northridge, a big earthquake hit our area in 1994. It hit in the middle of the night. It was such a shock. Since we were sound asleep, it took a while to figure out what was happening. Did a gas line burst? Were we being bombed? I was aware of Mary rolling over on top of me as glass was shattering all around us from the large windows we had installed above our bed. As in my ongoing nightmare, I could do nothing. We waited. The aftershocks continued to come. The electricity was out and we could literally not see our hands in front of our faces! It was pitch black. Water lines were broken and the earth was heaving. Eventually, Bob and his wife Sue came frantically pounding on our door to make sure we were both okay and to figure out what could be done. We decided it would be safer to get out of the house and into the RV. Fortunately, we had the RV. Unfortunately, it was parked a couple of miles away in a storage lot. Bob and Sue stayed with me while a friend drove Mary to get the RV and bring it back to our house. They helped get me out of the house, into my chair, and into the RV. I remember Mary running back to get my supplies: catheter, corset, leg bag, and anything else she could think of that I would need during the next few days. We remained relatively safe for the remainder of the night. The tires rolled a little, but they also cushioned the aftershocks that continued for a couple of days afterward.

When the shaking and tremors finally ceased, our newly remodeled home was full of broken vases, pictures, glass, cracked tile and walls, and damaged furniture. There was dust from the quake that had now turned to mud, because it was also flooded. The contents of every cupboard were in the midst of the chaos. Someone had tried to turn the water off, but in spite of their best efforts, the flooding continued.

Like everyone else in the area, we eventually found a contractor and a crew to clean up the mess and begin the repairs. Mary was so upset that we had lost so much; she was running here and there telling the workmen to stay away from the flower beds and don't step on the plants. Finally, the foreman came to me and said, "David, do you think you can get Mary out of here while we work?" I don't think, that with all the work they had to get done, saving the flowers was high on their priority list!

$85,000 and four months later, amazingly, the damage was repaired and the house was back in order. Nevertheless we broached the subject of moving. Where would we go?

Arizona was a logical place to start. It was close enough to visit family when we wanted to, and it was warm.

16

EVERYBODY'S HOMETOWN

IN THE SEARCH of a new place to call home, we took the RV, and an attendant, and headed to Tucson. Tucson was too hot for a quadriplegic, so we moved on to Phoenix, which was also too hot and too Los Angeles-like crowded. I remembered reading about a little town north of Phoenix called Prescott, only two hours away, but much cooler in the summer. I think it was one of the top 10 cities mentioned for retirement-minded people. We stayed at Forest Villas Hotel in Prescott while looking around. It was the only hotel at the time with a roll-in shower.

We inquired of people in Prescott where they suggested we look for homes or land and were directed to Williamson Valley. I waited in the van (adapted for wheelchairs) while Mary got out and scanned the lots. She evidently fell in love with the area on Twin Oaks Court and with one particular lot. As she walked back to the van, she told me, "It is just so peaceful. I think this is it." I looked at Mary and said, "I will do everything I can to get that land for you." We looked up the real estate agent to put an offer on the property, only to discover there were five people ahead of us with offers!

Unbelievable. In the middle of nowhere, and there were already five offers ahead of us? We put our offer in anyway and headed back to Northridge, disappointed. Two weeks later, our agent called and said the property was ours if we still wanted it. And that is how we came to live in Prescott, Arizona—Everybody's Hometown!

We bought 2.5 acres. Later, as we were building, the 5 acres behind us came on the market. Our contractor suggested this would be a great buy if we could do it. No one would ever build behind us. So we dug deep and bought the other 5 acres.

John Nanke was our building contractor and his brother Todd was our architect. We hired them in 1994. Todd owned a plane and surveyed our property from many angles. He and I came up with a plan that would work for my specific needs. Part of the property was in a flood zone, so the house had to be positioned in the best spot for rain run-off.

Barry Cohen went to bat for us again with the insurance company to get us an oversize bathtub and a Hoyer lift that was built into the ceiling joist of our bedroom. We needed tile floors as the wheelchair literally shreds carpets; and extra wide hallways, a roll-in shower, and flat thresholds. It took three years of planning before we were able to break ground in 1997. I had very specific ideas about what I wanted in my study and home theater, so I took my time designing them. They were not a part of the original bid.

Also, in 1997, we sold our house in Northridge. We stayed at the Point of Rocks campground in Prescott and advertised for an attendant who lived in the area. That is when we were fortunate enough to meet David P. Peterson, who would become our aide for many years to come. David was an EMT, a nurse, and is now a fire captain. He is the only one of our attendants who observed, "It's not everyone who meets his future employer nude and in a campground!"

When we finally made it to Twin Oaks Court, Mary drove the motorhome onto a cement pad we had built for that purpose. We stayed in the motorhome for the next six and a half months until the little guest house was finished. It was nice to move into the guest house. Even though it was tiny, it did have a roll-in shower and all the conveniences of a home. We stayed there another six and a half months until the house was finally ready. In May 1998, we moved into our new home—the day after it was ready! After all this time, it was a little scary moving into a large home.

The cost of medical care rose annually, and my medical needs were increasing with my age. For a while Barry got the insurance company to get us a new van every five plus years. It cost $50,000 to have it built to accommodate my chair. A new electric chair cost $33,000, and we wore one out every 5 years or so. Some people never got one. Barry was our champion! I needed to be strapped into a standing table to maintain my bone density. Barry made sure I got the table and an adapted stationary bike to exercise the upper part of my body. It was necessary to maintain what slight shoulder movement I had. The corsets I wore to hold me upright in my chair were $500, and I needed two each year.

I have to make it clear that the insurance company only paid for injury related assistance. We hired a great money manager. Mary did all she could to defray costs. With what we saved by Mary taking on part of my care, we invested well and made our own money for down payments, building, and personal needs. Otherwise, we would have spent every dime just for attendants, twenty-four hours a day. We loved our new home, and it didn't take long to become part of this great Prescott community.

Invocation for nursing students at Yavapai College.

17

A DAY IN MY LIFE

PEOPLE OFTEN ASK ME how I live my life. What is my day like? Imagine being left by yourself and you want to do something besides read. Imagine yourself taking a pair of 6 oz. boxing gloves with the thumbs sewn together. Now attached, they flop back and forth so there is no way to brace them. Now, further imagine picking up a glass, or turning over a tape in the cassette player, or flipping a page. That is what my life is like. It takes most of the day to do anything; and then it has to be done again or picked up off the floor by someone else!

***

I attended a friend's wedding. I needed to leave the reception to change my leg bag, so I asked my six-year-old nephew, also David, to push me outside to the restroom. He did, and right into a little ravine-like ditch. He was very upset, so I told him to go back into the reception and get someone to help me. He left and never came back! Much later, someone noticed I was missing and found me stuck in the ditch. When I asked little David why he didn't get someone to come and help me? He said, "Everyone was having fun and no one would listen to me, so I sat down and ate dinner."

***

Mary dropped me off at the movie theater. The movie was not her cup of tea, so she took me inside and got me situated and arranged to pick me up when the movie was over. I had a plastic tray on which to rest my arms. Mary put the wheelchair in the back row next to the first seat. In those days, there were no provisions for wheelchairs, so mine stuck out in the aisle. She attached the plastic tray and set a Coke and a bag of popcorn on it. I had a little more flexibility back then, so I could eat popcorn and lift a cup to my lips with both hands together. Every time movie goers walked into the theater, they bumped into my chair. I managed to keep the Coke upright until the movie started. Yeah! Success. When I tried to pick up the cup, my wrists failed me and the soda dropped onto the popcorn—another day in the life of David. When Mary arrived to pick me up, I was covered in soda and popcorn. I just hate that.

***

Another day in the life of David had me going for a "walk" in my motorized wheelchair. I thought the chair felt different than usual, but I left anyway. I treasured my time outside in the sun, and I often went on short excursions. Sometimes I took my dogs. Other times, it was just me. Our neighborhood was a lovely little community. I knew a lot of the people, and many of them knew of me. I left my house, turned left on Twin Oaks Drive, then left again for a short jaunt down Shadyoaks Drive. There were no sidewalks, so I was on the side of the street. As I approached Debi and Christian Deloof's house, the back of my motorized chair began to inch down. Lower and lower it went until my chair had tipped backwards; and I was still belted in, lying on my back in the street. I called out for help, but no one heard me. After a short time (I knew it was a short time because Mary timed my walks and would come looking for me if I was really late), Debi happened to be walking outside, saw me, and said, "David! What are you doing?" I replied, "Well, as long as I am down here, I thought I'd get a suntan."

"And the Beat Goes On"

- Sonny Bono

The very same thing happened when we went out to dinner at Red Lobster. This time, I had no inkling the chair's back would betray me. Mary helped me out of our van and into the restaurant where the waitress seated us in a room by ourselves. It was after the lunch rush and before dinner, so there was no one else in our section. Mary went off to the restroom and when she returned, I heard, "David, where are you?" "Down here," I replied. "Just looking at ceiling tiles again."

***

Another day, we decided to go to Sears for one reason or another. Mary wheeled me out of the van to where I could sit in the sun and wait for her. She attached a plexiglass tray across the arm rests so I had a place to put my arms. She set a cup of soda on the tray for me to drink while she popped into Sears. As I was waiting for her, minding my own business, a woman walked by and dropped a quarter in my cup. What! In my soda cup! She thought me to be a beggar? Did she not see my straw?

Had enough?

Me too!

18

YES! YOUR BRUSH CAN PAINT

I HAD A TRAINED HANDICAP DOG named Duke, and Mary had a buff-colored dog named Lizzie. Mary would attach their leashes to my electric chair and I would take them for a walk every day when the weather was favorable. It was on such a walk that I met neighbors John and Tom. Tom Jorden was a commercial artist, and he somehow determined I could draw. He decided he would teach me HOW I could do it. Tom taped chalk to my fingers, and we began trying to coordinate my brain and shoulders.

For hours, days, and weeks, I practiced making circles with my one good shoulder. When I mastered circles, I graduated to triangles, and then to squares. My OCD served me well. I was unstoppable. "Mary, if you could just come and change colors... brushes...move the easel...." I tried chalk, pencil, watercolors, acrylics, and oils. The oils didn't dry quickly enough and I smeared them easily. I eventually settled on a mixed media.

Our wonderful neighbors took notice and were very helpful. Mary bought a wrist brace, and Daryl Mathern fitted it with a device to hold brushes and pens. We hired two engineers to make an easel that could be moved up and down and sideways, since I couldn't. They put paints in those little daily pill boxes and hooked up a water mister to blow gently over the paints to prevent them from drying out. David Gilkerson came every Friday at 9 a.m. to change brushes, change colors, clean brushes— whatever I required.

Friend Tom getting David started.

At his desk at home.

"Blue Lion"

"Grandpa Reading a Letter"

From landscape collection.

From still life collection.

"Old Barn"

From Native American collection.

From still life collection.

"Old Cowboy"

From Jazz collection.

From women's collection.

19

DAILY LIFE

BILL MCMAHAN was my physical therapist for 23 years. He came to our house twice a week to stretch my muscles, strap me into the standing table, and work my shoulder on the exercise bike, among other things. We became such good friends that I jokingly introduced him by pointing out, "He is so effective; I was walking when we started therapy! Look where we are now." Bill eventually brought his wife, and later, his two daughters, Kelsey and Kenna, along to the house with him. We adored their little girls and loved to babysit them. We were honored and excited to become their godparents. Little Kenna talked like on old Southern woman with a deep, slow voice. Once I asked her if I could play a game with her. "NOOOOO! You in a wheel chaiyah," she cried.

Other Things to Keep Mary Busy

Monday was movie day. Every Monday at 1:00 p.m., I opened our home movie theater to avid neighborhood moviegoers. Jack, Christian, Tom, John, Tim, Bob, Bob, and Gaylord were regulars for movie and popcorn afternoons. It was a time for good male bonding, plus, we could watch war movies. I had literally a thousand movies from which to choose.

Church was a big part of our life. We looked until we found a wonderful church where we felt we fit in, and we loved the pastor.

We chose the Unity Church of Prescott, because the people were so friendly and very supportive.

I was desperate not to miss out on anything, so naturally, I had to fly in a glider, zip on a zip line, and float in a hot air balloon. You really have to stop and visualize what it takes to accomplish these feats! The chair went with me and together we weighed in at 600 lbs.

I also trained local nurses on how to care for quadriplegic and paraplegic patients. I was always happy to give motivational speeches. I kept busy and I kept Mary busy. We lived life to its fullest.

Happy for a ride.

David's 50th birthday, in our backyard in California.

Feeding my best friend, an "every" meal joy.

Camping with our adapted RV.

Hot Air Balloon Ride, Palm Springs

David reading to children at the library in Prescott.

Helping on Laundry Day.

Toastmasters... ready to give a speech.

The three brothers: Jim, David and Bob.

Walking both dogs at once.

Friends.

Our first service dog, James.

Loving My Sweetheart.

20

THINGS I'VE LEARNED

Quality in Quality Out

I BELIEVE, and taught, that each one of us needs to be accountable and responsible in everything we do. If we can give ourselves that beautiful gift in a loving, non-judgmental way, then it is a snap to give responsibility and accountability, wrapped in a beautiful bow, to others. In my own life experience, I cannot tell you how free I feel from the burdens of my own self-inflicted negativity: that has kept me from showing my own flaws and perceived unsavory character issues. You become more human and relatable to others when you can be candid as you continue working on your shortcomings. It seems to be a lifelong endeavor.

Each one of us has the power to make a difference in ourselves and others. That is where real success lies. It lies in being of service to others. Indirectly, we also give love and purpose to ourselves. It's such a good deal! If you can hold five positive thoughts that you never had before, and keep holding on to them, over time, those seemingly inconsequential thoughts will make magnificent changes in your life direction.

So often, we see the roadblocks and we say, "I don't know how I can even do this." Just look around you. There are lots of people who have done it. They are not smarter than you; they are not richer than you; but they figured it out. You will too.

"You Must Learn from The Mistakes of Others.
You Cannot Possibly Live Long Enough to
Make Them All Yourself."

- Sam Levenson

After 17 years of practice, I was surprised to find there are some people worse off than I am. These are the people who are trapped in the prison of their own minds. Able-bodied, but consumed with fear, paranoia, and madness. I never thought 40 years ago that I would envy my life over theirs. I hope I helped them. They all helped me. At the end of every day, I thanked God for my life, and I thanked God for my mind. I thank all those people who have been in my life: The ones who've been supporting me, and also the ones who have been my challenge, because those have helped me "keep my ass in one saddle" and stay on the right course. Thank you to all of you.

"What we focus on is what we become. That is old stuff," said my friend W. H. Mitchell. But there is no new stuff! We do the old stuff because that is what works. We all say, "Garbage in, garbage out." How about we change that to, "Quality in, quality out?" Let's say what we want to happen.

Mary calls my emotionally down days, my cripple days. I have accumulated a vast library of motivational videos and books. I have developed a history or pattern of self-help that I use whenever I feel sorry for myself. I watch one of the videos or read one of the books to pull myself out of the gloom. I believe the constant reinforcement is what enables people to be successful. Instead of focusing on the 9000 things I can no longer do, I focus on the 1000 things I can do, and I am grateful.

"Only Those Who Care About You
Can Hear You When You Are Quiet."

- Kushandwizdom

I have learned that we grow through crisis. There are times when we are stretched to the limit, when our back is against the wall, and we have had some extremely painful experience. Afterward, we realize that without those experiences, we wouldn't have manifested the kinds of qualities and understanding we now possess.

Still to this day, I get asked to call on or speak to newly injured patients and others faced with truly terrible challenges. I have learned so much, and I always want to help them. I have also learned that they must be receptive. Remember, I was angry and in denial for upwards of six years. I have found, as with myself, that people must be at the point of asking themselves, "What can I do? Instead of asking, "Why did this happen to me?" I don't have to tell them that I understand. They can look at me and see the situation I've lived with for over 50 years. So instead, I reach out with my heart, my eyes, and my voice to tell them how much it stinks—it just sucks. We can agree on that. I join their reality as I would with any of my psychotic patients. We don't try to change their reality, we join in. It's called empathy.

I have learned that it is easier to convince people you have pain if they can see it. People can look at me and know I have a problem. I feel sorry for people with internal pain or issues. They are not so lucky. They can be accused of faking it. It is very difficult for them.

My philosophy on learning: It is possible to learn quickly, but not probable. People only use a small percentage of their brain. It really has to do with the depth and degree of how much we allow these truths and ideas to penetrate—to actually become part of us. For most of us, it takes different people at different times and in different ways to keep saying the same thing over and over to us until we get it. That is why there is such a great demand for more speakers to share ideas, educate, stimulate, and motivate. Sometimes it takes just the right words, or just the right person to deliver those words. Then the timing must be right. Finally, we must always be receptive.

There are probably only 50 major truths relating to success and healthy relationships that can be found in the Bible and other books of wisdom. We have to take them in repeatedly until they find a way to stick.

Gaining insight from different perspectives is the only process that I believe has helped me understand ways in which I can expand my ability to be of service to others. Speaking is one of them, writing is another, teaching is another, and counseling is another.

Now, I just tell people, "When you have been hit your hardest blow, just stand up and say, 'Ta-Da! I'm still here! I am still standing!'"

Over the years, I've received lots of commentary notes from patients. I've kept them all in a separate file. I have read them from time to time, and still do, to remind me of my purpose, and that I was making a difference.

21

PERSONAL REFLECTIONS

I HAVE BEEN MARRIED THREE TIMES. I've always had difficulty with relationships. How do you know who is the right one? My first wife was a wonderful girl with good values. I wasn't sure she was the right one, but I did feel that if I didn't marry her, I would lose her. At 22, most of my friends were getting married. I felt coerced, either by my friends, my girlfriend, or even myself. On the second day of our honeymoon, I remember looking out the window as a sick feeling came over me. I said to myself, as I pressed my fist into my hand, "What the heck have you done?" I was terrified. I was always a sucker for a beautiful woman. Maybe that was my Achilles heel.

I was married to my second wife for a very short, ill-conceived period of time. She was a psychiatric patient of mine. I couldn't believe anyone would marry me again. She was Hollywood glamorous, and I thought I could make her well. I couldn't.

Now I have a wonderful relationship with my wife Mary. She's beautiful, she's attractive, and she has wonderful social skills. She helps me move ahead and magnifies the success of my profession in every way. Every day, and I say this honestly, I let her know how much I appreciate what she has meant to me and all that she does for me. Most of the time, it may be in words, or a touch, or a hug; but in other ways, too. Our relationship lifts me to new levels that I would never have experienced without her. Mary taught me about love. She didn't need protection. She didn't need fixing. She accepted me as I was.

At the end of the day, what really matters is that your loved ones are safe, you've done your best, and that you are thankful for what you have.

22

THE DECEMBER OF MY DAYS

IN AUGUST 2019, at Mary's request, the neighbors set up a telephone relay to pass the word that I had gone on hospice at my house. If anyone wanted to say goodbye, now would be a good time, as I was still feeling up to having visitors. My friends were warned to stay just a few minutes so as not to over tire me; there were a lot of friends! Some were awkward with the idea of death, so I comforted them. On one hand, I knew I was dying. On the other hand, I didn't give in to the idea at all.

Bob Lynn was at the house helping me go through some DVDs, and I told him I wanted to order new shoes. Evidently, he didn't know how to process that information, so he told Mary. Mary said, "David, Bob said you would like to order new shoes. Why do you think you need new shoes?" I said, "I have a lot more walking to do on this earth." At that point, I could have ordered five pairs of shoes! Bob ordered the shoes. When people came to see me and became too sad that I was on hospice, I would comfort them by saying, "Don't worry, I can't die, I have new shoes." Optimistic, always.

One day, Mary left for a while. Debbie Mathern and I usually watched Hallmark Christmas stories together when Mary was out. This time there were many other people at the house. When she returned, I asked her where she had been. She said she had been to the funeral home. I was not in the habit of asking where she goes, so she was caught off guard and told the truth. I said, "Not for me?"

One of my visitors was my neighbor, Carrie Palmer, an eighty-five-year-old who had been widowed for six years. We spoke in the shade of my back patio. I asked her what her biggest challenge was at this point in her life.

She said, "Grief."

I said, "Yes, that is the most difficult to deal with of all. I have so much more I would like to do before I am ready to go."

23

MARY LEMON

Meanwhile in Iowa...

HOW DO YOU DECIDE who you will marry? Are you attracted to a killer body, an extraordinary intellect, or a person from a foreign land? Are you intrigued by the essence one evokes in you of a prior love? Do you seek someone with the same interests, or do you fall for someone with no shared interests at all? Only you can make that decision. My name is Mary and this is my story.

Against my family's better judgement, I married David Van Gorder, a handsome, pleasant, caring man—and much to their distress and concern—also a quadriplegic. It was September 28, 1991 when we married and settled into wedded bliss in a house we bought in Northridge, California.

Maybe "distress" is a little harsh—maybe not. But they were all worried about me. Worried about my ability to handle such an extreme and demanding lifestyle—for the rest of my life!

My older sister Suzanne and I were born in Waterloo, Iowa. We were raised by my parents, Russ and Lena.

I seemed to always have a soft spot in my heart for those who were down and out or suffering on some level. My dad wasn't well for about three years, and no one could figure out why. I was very sensitive to his situation. Eventually, I decided to become a licensed vocational nurse. I attended Hawkeye Technical School and passed the test for my license. It would be weeks before the license was issued. In the meantime, I had met a nice young man who encouraged me to go to California. I wanted to go, but my dad was pretty much against it. So, as young women do, I went.

The young man lived by the beach in Marina Del Ray, but his parents lived inland in Hacienda Heights. He said that his parents would be happy to take me in and give me a hand until I received my license and was able work as a nurse. They were such kind people. Nothing ever came of a relationship with their son, but I was forever grateful for the generosity of his parents! His mom got me a part-time job at the County Road Department. While working there, I met my first husband, John Sholtis, who was a civil engineer in the same building. He asked me to help him use the copy machine. The next day, a lady I worked with told me, "Mary, John has worked here for years. He knows how to use the copy machine!"

"At Some Point You Have to Let Go of The Life You Wanted and Start Living the Life You Have."

- Unknown

Three months later, John and I were engaged. Three months after the engagement, we were married in Waterloo, Iowa. By that time, my father had finally been diagnosed with colon cancer. I wanted my dad to give me away. John was thoughtful enough to drive with his best man to my hometown so this could happen.

I was 10 years younger than John. In my eyes, he was a man of the world. We honeymooned for an entire month up and down the East Coast. It was wonderful! John owned a home in the Hollywood Hills, and that is where we lived for the next four years. Our daughter Angela was born in 1971, two years after we were married. Ours was not a neighborhood with a lot of children, mostly adults and a lot of movie people. There were a lot of steps in our hillside home on the side of a mountain. Angela stumbled down most of them. So when Angela was two, we bought a "flatter" house in Van Nuys. Three years and nine months later, Angela's brother Shawn, was born. As the children got older, I took a part-time job at a center for kids with alcohol and drug addiction, and various mental problems. By that time, our marriage was unraveling. We had been married almost 20 years.

I eventually got an apartment and signed up with a placement agency that sent me to various hospitals and doctor's offices to fill in on a temporary basis. I saw our children on the weekends, and we all managed the best we could under the circumstances.

I had a girlfriend with Muscular Dystrophy who was having trouble dressing herself, so I signed up for a patternmaking class at UCLA to see if I could figure out how to make clothes more suited to her needs. I spent a year researching how to make handicap clothing.

"Everyone You Meet Is Fighting a Battle
You Know Nothing About. Be Kind. Always"
- Robin Williams

About this time, I was hired for temporary work at Pasadena Community Hospital. I had been a psychiatric nurse for a few years by then, so I settled in easily. I was chatting with the nurses and telling them about my dear friend who had M.S. I was determined to make some clothing for her that would be easier to get on and off. I asked them if they had any suggestions. One of them said, "We have a disabled doctor in the hospital right now. Why don't you go in and see him?" So off I went, unknowingly, to meet the love of my life.

"Love Has Nothing to Do with What You Are
Expecting to Get- Only with What You Are Expecting
to Give, Which Is Everything."
- Katherine Hepburn

24

LOVE OF MY LIFE

I FOUND DR. VAN GORDER, or Dr. Dave as his patients called him, in the Psychiatric Ward. He was counseling a group of women who were addicted to alcohol or drugs. He invited me to sit in. It was obvious at first glance that the women absolutely adored and trusted him. Each one had bonded with him and understood that he knew what he was talking about. We spoke easily for a while, and he asked me if I would come to one of his classes, which I did. I began taking notes for him. Since he couldn't write, he always had to ask a nurse or an aide to "chart" for him. And not everyone was thrilled to do his work and their work, too.

We formed an easy friendship and often met for lunch in the hospital cafeteria. Even though I was a nurse who had cared for paralyzed patients, I really didn't know how they actually got through their day. David asked me to give him a bite of food, so I fed him. Easy peasy. A comfortable friendship was forming. My temporary status at the hospital was lengthened, and we continued to get to know each other better.

"You Don't Fall in Love with a Body,
You Fall in Love with a Soul,
And Once You Fall in Love with a Soul,
Everything About That Body Becomes Beautiful."

- A.B.

About two months into my term at the hospital, I was venting to anyone who would listen, including Dr. Dave, about my pending divorce. I was in a lot of pain and needed an outlet. I had been married for 20 years. It was a very difficult ending for me. At one point, Dr. Dave told me, "Mary, everyone here is getting a little tired of hearing about your divorce. I will listen to you for 10 more minutes, then we won't mention it again." So we moved on to other topics, looking forward to the future, and left the past where it belonged, behind us, for then.

One day, as Dr. Dave was preparing to teach a class, his bowels let loose. Quadriplegics have no control of their bowels and it can happen anytime. I said, "I'll call an aide and we can get you cleaned up and ready for your class." David said, "No, I made the mess, I'll just sit in it till the end of the day." Of course, he was embarrassed and certainly didn't want me to see him so helpless and dependent. In my practical way, I just said, "Nonsense, I will have an aide bring you clean clothes and we will deal with this in the other room." And that is what we did. I believe it broke down a barrier of sorts between us. He now understood that I wasn't put off by his situation. We continued our friendship and eventually began dating.

I was sitting next to David one afternoon, and I put my hand on his thigh. I said, "David, I have my hand on your leg." He said, "I know. I can feel it in my heart." Now tell me, how could you not love a man like that?

This was 1989. I still hadn't made any handicap clothing.

"Being Deeply Loved by Someone Gives You Strength, While Loving Someone Deeply Gives You Courage"

- Lao Tzu

25

OUR HISTORY ACCORDING TO MARY

WE WERE NEVER APART after Pasadena Community Hospital. When it lost funding, I went with him wherever we could find work. Our next assignment was at Pine Grove Psychiatric Hospital, Encino, California. At Pine Grove, David taught classes for abused and battered women. It was the first program of its kind, and David was excited to teach it. Additionally, he continued working with patients in the garage office at his parents' house. I took on the job of his office manager in charge of billables and payables. Not my strongest suit, but I did my best for David, as always.

From the beginning, we spoke openly and freely with one another, and agreed never to play games or hurt each other on purpose. No threatening to leave or making the other jealous. Just be honest and forthright. I knew he had down days, and he knew I needed to eat—and on time! Low blood sugar or something like that. Everyone who knew me knew I wasn't happy when I was hungry! We worked together every day and managed well.

We bought a house in Northridge, across the street from his brother and down the street from his dad. He still didn't think I would stay with him very long, so he wanted to be close to his family. One day, we drove downtown to a jewelry store where he asked me pick out an engagement ring! I have reminded him since then that he has never proposed to me.

We set a wedding date. I was determined to make our back yard the most beautiful site I could for our special day. I planted flowers with the most vibrant colors I could find.

The wedding was wonderful, and the yard was so gorgeous; I was so proud of it. I loved having everyone with us, enjoying our little Garden of Eden, until David decided we should all go into the garage and do Karaoke. So much for my beautiful yard. You never knew what David was going to do next.

I was always fit, but I started getting up at 5 a.m. to go to the gym to work out. I had to remain strong enough to pick David up each day. That was my contribution. I also started researching the best diet for him.

Squirrel Cheeks

One thing I learned about David: David loved to eat! One time, I was feeding him popcorn. I was being so careful. I didn't want him to choke, so I was feeding him one kernel at a time. Finally, he said, "Mary, hurt me when you feed me!" He could eat a LOT at once. His nieces and nephews loved to feed him and see how much they could fit in his mouth at one time. We used to call him "Squirrel Cheeks". He didn't like to ask people to feed him, so he put as much as possible in his mouth with each bite.

I never told David what he could or couldn't eat, but I provided us with what I thought we needed in the way of a balanced diet, along with good supplements. Once when we were out to dinner with Jerry and his daughter Chamile, I left the room for a few minutes. I heard David say to Jerry," Quick, feed me cake. Don't tell Mary!" Chamile was distressed and yelled, "Dad, stop! You're going to choke him!" David was a pistol!

Another time, we were out to dinner with friends and the waitress, assuming David was deaf in addition to the obvious, turned to me and asked me what David would like for dinner. Without missing a beat, I turned to David, gesticulating wildly with my fingers, and mouthing the words, "David, what would you like to eat?" The entire table found this to be hilarious. When the waitress asked the woman next to David if she would like a cocktail, after we had all ordered one, she said, "No." David, busy being David, said, "What? Are you Mormon or something?" She said, "Why, yes." Comedy was not his calling.

My children, Angela and Shawn, had a difficult time going through my divorce from their father. David never tried to be a replacement father, but told them how lucky they were to have the benefit of TWO fathers! David answered all of their questions, no matter how personal, without flinching. They liked that he was always interested in them and paid close attention all the time. Occasionally, one of my children would get a call from David saying, "This is your evil step-father. Call your mother!" David taught them never to hesitate to ask for help. While on a family cruise, David was trying to navigate the streets of a third-world (ish) country and noticed a sheet of metal covering a manhole. He asked Shawn to see if he could pick it up so it could be used as a ramp to get David up and over the curb. Shawn did and then was assigned to carry that metal piece around town the rest of the day!

After the earthquake in Northridge in 1994, we bought land in Prescott, Arizona. We lived in our motorhome during the design and construction of our house. It was a long-term project, so we had to have the motorhome outfitted with a lift so I could get David in and out of bed. It was like a jump line you might be harnessed into to glide over tree tops in a jungle on an exotic vacation. I (or an aide when we could get one) would fit the harness around David, followed by much rolling to the left and then rolling to the right, since he couldn't be lifted straight up. That is also how I got him dressed, rolling to the left, then rolling to the right, until he was sufficiently put together in street clothes. David cared about how he looked. He did not want to look like anything other than a healthy, well-dressed, and well-groomed man, even while living in a motorhome. The lift had a manual lever much like a water pump. I would pump it until it lifted him up and I could either get him dressed or into his chair so I could get him into the bathroom to begin his daily ablutions. David's entire morning process took three hours each day.

We advertised for another attendant and were lucky to find James Ledgerwood. James came along on RV trips with us. He was such a nice, easy going guy.

**

We were living in Prescott. David was going to attend a function at which he was to speak. He had set his heart on wearing his brand-new, custom-made, ostrich skin boots. He was so excited when they were delivered on the day of the event. He really wanted to wear them that night. They were beautiful and very expensive. He had no muscle to push his foot into the boots, so they were made with large zippers that went all the way to the bottom of the boot. When they arrived, he immediately wanted to try them on. After much pushing and maneuvering by me, David said, "I think they are too tight. Maybe James would wear them around for a couple of hours today and stretch them out for me." After a side bet involving an In and Out Burger, James, ever the sport, agreed. James was a tall man and wore a size 12 shoe; David wore a size 10. Ouch! Nevertheless, James gamely walked the walk—like a cowboy who had been robbed of his horse and boots and had to walk painfully back into town on whatever part of his foot didn't have a blister. I actually heard him counting the minutes until he could remove them, "12 more minutes, 11 more minutes…" until he was done. Boots, sufficiently stretched; David was clean, dressed, and ready for boots. Then, at the last minute he decided not to wear them.

"You Will Find That You Don't Need to Trust Others as Much as You Need to Trust Yourself to Make the Right Choices. "

- Don Miguel Ruiz

***

We had lots of adventures with our friends. Pete and Susie took us to see Montezuma's Castle. There was a steep, narrow pathway leading up to the castle cliff dwelling. It was a good thing Pete was strong enough to hold David's wheelchair, or David would have traveled the narrow, downhill path all by himself!

***

Prescott Center for the Arts is located on Marina Street in an historic Catholic church. There were many steep, prohibitive steps leading up to the front door. Also, there was a rickety and very old elevator on the side of the building that would only hold one person at a time. It had started to snow when we put David in the elevator; the door ever so slowly began to close. The exertion was too much for the old lift. David weighed in at 250 pounds, and his chair weighed 350 pounds. When the elevator rose three inches off the ground, it stopped. Period. The caretakers said, "Don't worry, we will call the elevator people to come in from Chino Valley and open it." Panicked, David railed, "#&^% that *^&%! Call 911." Being stuck in a chair AND in an elevator the size of a coffin, in the snow, was just too much for him to bear. The 911 crew appeared post haste, opening the door with a crowbar and freeing David straightaway. There is now a wheelchair ramp at the side door. A plaque, inscribed with the names of grateful art donors, including ours, hangs on the wall next to the new ramp.

***

That reminds me; I believe there is an outhouse somewhere in Uganda, Africa, that has a plaque on it dedicated to us. My best friend Wendy spent many years in Uganda. We were touched by the story of a young boy who lost his legs by being run over by a train. Upon hearing of his struggles to use a latrine, we paid to have a custom latrine built so the boy could have a measure of dignity while using the restroom. We were evidently the stuff of legends in Uganda for that act of kindness and for the confidence we had in a person with disabilities. People with disabilities in Uganda are totally dismissed as worthless. One thoughtful act gave the young man a feeling of self-worth. Over the years, David encouraged him to get artificial legs, even though it would be a long, painful process.

David counseled another young man from Uganda. He told him, regarding his troublesome girlfriend, "You could marry her, but it will be an uphill battle to love her." The young man decided to wait until he could find a "Mary" of his own, just like David did.

***

We built "Camp David" in back of our house. It was a fun area to have friends over for BBQ's and pot luck dinners. I celebrated my 60th birthday there with our friends and neighbors. We both loved to socialize, but David was the King. He loved to talk with people. There was always a crowd around him. Barney Logan observed that David always had the best seat in the house; he was always surrounded by friends! David and I were regular attendees at neighborhood gatherings as well. David preferred to host parties because it was easier for him to be at home in his chair in familiar surroundings. Unless the dinner was outside, it took a small army to get him up steps and through narrow doorways into others' homes. Debbie Mathern loved David so much that she refused to have an indoor party that he could not attend due to his chair!

***

Next to Camp David, we created Mary's Garden; so noted by a cute sign that reads, "Mary's Garden." I tried my hand at growing fresh, organic vegetables—tried being the operative word. You would think a girl from Iowa would have better luck, but I failed at gardening. I couldn't even grow lettuce.

115

I belong to a monthly coffee group in our neighborhood. Every six weeks I collect "Green Bags" full of food from our group, then donate to the local food cupboards. We are specifically interested in the "No Hungry Kids" program. We were shocked to discover how many school-aged children are homeless or go without food! Our generous neighbors are always at the top of the list of donors. I am thrilled that my grandson now enjoys accompanying me to deliver the food to the distribution center.

***

Even though I had a lot on my plate, or maybe because of it, I did have a sense of humor—strange, funny, and accidental. At a doctor's appointment, I explained to my doctor, in all seriousness, "You know, I have osteo*penis*, don't you?"

***

While walking his dogs, David ran into our neighbors John and Tom. Tom happened to be an artist. After a conversation, Tom determined he could teach David to paint. Two optimistic people! As our friend Elizabeth Harris said, "David knew how to wring every bit of good out of life." Thus, began David's new career as an artist. Our neighbors rallied around and helped David set up an art studio and then volunteered to come help him change brushes, prepare gesso boards, and mix colors. David Gilkason was one of them. He did whatever David's heart desired, including making phone calls. My David was always afraid he was going to die and didn't want to miss out on anything. When David thought he needed something, he needed it right now! David had an ongoing list of things he wanted, and David G. was willing to place the orders…but, "You can't tell Mary!" Who did my David think paid the bills? The other David, David G., was, and still is, a gem and settled only for lunch in exchange for all of his time and dedication.

"Art Demands Constant Observation."

- Vincent Van Gogh

David tried taking art lessons at Phippin Museum and a couple of other places in town, but the hauling around of David, his easels, paints, misters, etc. became too much for me, so we decided it would be easier to have teachers come to the house. Clairene Barrett was one of the most excellent instructors of them all. Like Dr. Bloom, she made him "walk the walk," so to speak.

It was painful watching him practice circles for hours on end, until he could move on to triangles! In time, David became very skilled at painting, but on occasion, had to call in other artists for the fine-tune work, like the eyes, if he was painting a person. Ultimately, David created hundreds of paintings and sold at least half of them at the Mountain Artists Guild art shows on the square in downtown Prescott, the 'Tis art center and gallery, and the Art2 Prescott gallery. He relied on other artists less as he became better and better. David loved beautiful things and learned to express the beauty in his life through his art.

***

We both joined Toastmasters when we moved to Prescott. David loved to talk, and talk, and talk. We attended weekly meetings on Wednesday afternoons. There was a job for everyone. Sometimes, you were given a subject about which to write. Sometimes, you were the bell ringer, other times the fact checker. Everyone had something to do to keep them engaged. David would wait until the last minute to prepare. I would have to look up pages and pages of research while trying to prepare my own speech. The speeches were slated to last from 3-5 minutes, depending upon the subject. When it was David's turn to talk, he couldn't stop. People loved him and didn't mind his 15-minute extrapolations. Except, once, when he was invited to speak at a graduation ceremony.

David was the current president of the Prescott Area Leadership Club. He was asked to give the opening salutation. David always had so much knowledge to impart, he sometimes failed to notice his audience couldn't take in that much wisdom. During his discourse, David stopped speaking and announced a short break, after which he would continue his opening remarks. During the break almost half of the audience took the opportunity to slide on down the road to the after parties. It was awkward!

26

IF YOU COULD JUST...

WHEN DAVID AND I BEGAN TO DATE, I would spend time with him after his aide got him ready for bed. When it was time for me to leave, it was, "Mary, if you could... just get me this," or "Mary, if you could... just get me that." I had to tell him, "You have 10 more minutes, then I have to leave." The whole point of our little dance was that he really didn't want me to leave at all.

When we married, David told me he would always be grateful for me and for all I did for him. I thought it was just "newly married" promises that would fall by the wayside in time. Not so. David was grateful. He showed it, or said it, or gave me things every day. David bought me flowers, he painted me pictures, gave me gold panning lessons (I forgave him eventually), and did any number of things he could think to do, including just saying thank you. I felt very loved and appreciated. It was a hard life, but it was a good life.

I had a lot of empathy for David. I saw how he struggled every day. I often told him that I would willingly trade places with him and be a quadriplegic in his place for a day so he could have a break. I meant it. I would love to have been able to give him that gift of relief from his confinement. He just smiled.

In spite of the: "If you could just... do this," "get that, "move this," David was the love of my life. I would do anything for him. At the end of each day, however, I was flat out tired. I was done. I would go through the process of getting David into bed. "Anything else, David? Are you comfortable? Is your pillow in the proper place? OK then, I'm exhausted. I'm getting into bed and going to sleep." Eyes closing, then, I would hear, "Mary?"

#$@&%!...* I thought—in the spirit of love, of course.

27

HEALTH ISSUES

IT WAS ALWAYS THE GOOD—and the difficult. Quadriplegics suffer from spasticity. The muscles in their arms or legs constrict and jump unbidden. Everything from cold weather, to tight shoes, to nothing at all causes it to happen. I'm sure many people thought I was being fresh with David when I pressed my hand on his legs!

We always had to be vigilant and catch little health issues before they became major health issues such as pneumonia, deep vein thrombosis (blood clots in the veins), pulmonary embolisms (blood clots in the lungs), contractures (shortening of the muscles and ligaments restricting movement), and decubitus (ulcers or bed sores caused by low or no blood flow). Autonomic dysreflexia is a mass reflex syndrome characterized by uncontrolled hypertension (high blood pressure) and bradycardia (low heart rate below 60 bpm); it is a full body response to something not working properly in the body. It can cause seizures and death. Even with all that daily care, quadriplegics were most likely to die from heart attacks.

In our early days together, we probably ended up in the emergency room four times a year. As time progressed, we were in the hospital so often that we referred to it as date night! We were grateful for every day and wary of the next. David counseled couples regularly. We were under a lot of stress, as you might imagine. The counseling sessions he taught, primarily on communication, also helped us to cope with our own problems of illness and injury.

In 2002, I made a cup of coffee and was walking across the kitchen floor when I froze. I was aware that I was standing still, but I couldn't talk, or move, or do anything. It lasted a minute or two, then I continued walking as if nothing had happened. I told David, "The oddest thing just happened to me." When I finished relating my story, he said, "Call Wendy and have her take you to the emergency room." I didn't think much of it and didn't want to go. So David asked an aide who was standing nearby to call my best friend Wendy. She came right over. An MRI confirmed I had had a stroke. The doctor could not immediately determine why I had a stroke, but he didn't give up. Six weeks later, I was sent to Phoenix and scheduled for surgery. I had been born with a hole in my heart and a blood clot had made it through to my brain. Other than a slightly tricky memory, I fully recovered.

That wasn't the end of my surprises for the decade. My back went out again in 2016. I was so worried. Who would take care of both of us? I just had to get better. It took weeks, but I had a great doctor and, once again, recovered with the help of my friends and neighbors.

We still weren't done. Life just kept coming at us. David woke up one morning in 2017 with a droopy eye and a weak arm (weaker than usual). We had no idea what to think of it, so began the round of doctors until one of them said, "I think it could be Myasthenia Gravis." This was the same disease that Aristotle Onassis had when he was married to Jackie Kennedy. We had never heard of it. There was no cure, but it could be managed with high doses of prednisone.

Prednisone has side effects. One of the side effects caused his skin to break down. David developed a huge sore on this thigh. It was called a bed sore. Bed sore sounds rather benign, but it is not. The sore became infected. By the time he had surgery, I could put my fist all the way through the wound and grab his bone. It was devastating.

*"I Wish I Could Turn Back the Clock...
I'd Find You Sooner and Love you Longer."*

- lessonslearnedinlife.com

David was prescribed bedrest 23 hours a day for 8 months! The wound was too large to stitch; it had to close up on its own. Movement was restricted to a minimum. We just could not have handled this new situation without our friends and neighbors. It was too overwhelming. Neighbors Mike and Mel Clune came to our house every day at nine o'clock in the morning for 8 straight months to get David out of bed, into his chair, and outside in the sun for an hour. While David begged to stay out longer, they followed doctor's orders to the letter.

At our eight-month follow-up appointment, we were disappointed. The wound was not healing well. At that point, the doctor told David, "I was a field surgeon during the war, and many young men had gaping wounds similar to yours. We just told them to go home and live the rest of their lives. That is what I am suggesting you do. Just go about living your life." That is what we did. Beneficial or not, staying in bed was not David's way.

Rusty, Christian, and Jack helped us with everything. Rusty, and a lady named Dita, took turns coming over in the evening to help David into bed.

28

DAVID'S LAST DAYS

DAVID WENT INTO HOSPICE CARE at our home in August 2019. It was unbearably sad watching everyone take their turns saying goodbye. There is a bell on our driveway that rings to alert us when a car drives to the house. It rang constantly, like the Bells of St. Mary's. David's brothers and other family came to be with him. The nieces and nephews said their goodbyes one at a time, and were each told they were special and loved. Shawn, Angela, Laurie, Andrus, and all of the grandchildren were inconsolable. They all loved "Bapa" so much.

> *"You Never Know How Strong You Are, Until*
> *Being Strong is Your Only Choice."*
> - Bob Marley

On September 26, 2019, David was in the shower chair in the bathroom getting ready for the day. Suddenly, he began screaming, "Get me out of here, Now! Get me into bed!" The very same unbearable, knife-like stabbing pain that he had felt right after his accident was back! Shortly after he was in bed, David fell into a coma. I put my chair right next to him and talked to him for a long time. I turned on a movie and just sat there with him. By the evening of the second day, I told him, "David, I have to rest for a little while." Then, I dozed off for an hour or so. When I awoke, David had passed. It was two days before our 28th wedding anniversary.

On the day of our anniversary, a bouquet of flowers arrived with the message: "Happy Anniversary from Heaven. Love, David". It was sent by my daughter Angela. She knew David that well. Her wonderful act of love will remain in my heart forever.

29

LOOKING BACK: THE BIG QUESTION, BY DAVID

NOW, THE ANSWER to the big question people want to know: After all you have accomplished during your life, would you have changed it if you could?

I would say I've had an extraordinary life. I have a beautiful, caring, and capable wife who loves me and cares for me, literally and figuratively. I am grateful for her every day of my life. I have a wonderful custom home on 7.5 acres that I envisioned myself and is everything I could dream. I have managed to attain a certain amount of status, by anyone's standards, having earned a doctorate in clinical psychology, something I still find difficult to believe. And because of that degree, I have been able to help people who were truly worse off than me. I have become a public speaker and was awarded the highest honor the National Speakers Association had to bestow. I have become an artist who, I am proud to say, has actually sold his paintings. I feel blessed to have step-children, grandchildren, nieces, nephews, and God children. I have met wonderful and helpful people from all over the globe. I have met others, not so wonderful, who have also been valuable to my growth. So, if I had a choice to do it all over again, would I? Or… would I choose to walk? Some in my position say they wouldn't change a thing. They have achieved so much more than they ever thought was possible, as have I.

If I had to answer honestly, I would have to say yes. Yes, I would choose to walk again. I have dreamed and hoped it would happen every day since I became paralyzed. I want to feel the grass under my bare feet. I want to brush my own teeth. I want to dance all night. I want to drive my own car again. I want to make love to my wife. I want to do a hundred other things that most people don't even think about until they can no longer do them. And I want to live each day without pain—there is always so much pain.

But, also, after all is said and done, I didn't have a choice to do it over again. My recovery was not dependent upon Deepak Chopra's teachings; my recovery was not dependent upon my parents' belief in those teachings; and it was never my choice, as diligently as I tried to recover. As my dear friend, W. Mitchell, said, "David, it is not what happens to you, it's what you do about it."

That was the only choice I ever had. I think I chose well.

Ultimately, my life has been about inspiring others to do better. I hope I have done that for you. I am grateful to every single one of you.

I'll see you on the other side.

- David Van Gorder

30

PROMISE ME

"Promise me you'll always remember: You're braver than you believe, and stronger than you seem, and smarter than you think."

- Christopher Robin to Winnie the Pooh (by A. A. Milne)

31

MEMORIAL

AT DAVID'S MEMORIAL, Reverend Tom Catlin, David's pastor, observed that the best part of David's life was Mary, and the best part of Mary's life was David. Love and humor permeated their lives and flowed through to all who knew them. He also said a good man never dies. He leaves a part of him in everyone that knew him. And so it was with David.

MEMORIAL POEM

I am standing upon the seashore. A ship at my side spreads her white sails to the morning breeze and starts for the blue ocean. She is an object of beauty and strength. I stand and watch her until at length as she hangs like a speck of white cloud just where the sea and sky come to mingle with each other. Then someone at my side says:

"There, she is gone!"

"Gone where?"

Gone from my sight. That is all. She is just as large in mast and hull and spar as she was when she left my side and she is just as able to bear the load of living freight to her destined port.

Her diminished size is in me, not in her. And just at the moment when someone at my side says: "There, she is gone!" There are other eyes watching her coming and other voices ready to take up the glad shout: "Here she comes!"

And that is dying…

- Henry Van Dyke

David (top) with brothers Jim (left) and Bob (right).

A WORD TO DAVID'S YOUNGEST GENERATION

DAVID WAS BORN May 22, 1943 in Van Nuys, California, at his grandfather's home. There were eight adults living together in the small house when David, the first grandson, made his debut. In Hebrew, David means *Beloved*. He was almost called Peter, which means *the Rock*. David always thought that Peter fit more with his personality. After waiting three days for his mother to decide what to name him, his aunt (God Bless her) named him David.

According to everyone, he was certainly spoiled. David was picked up, rocked, soothed and fed, and doted upon when the tiniest little squeak escaped his lips. With eight doting adults watching his every move, he was never left alone. David was the sun and the stars to his extended family, and I might add, quite happy with the situation. Two years later, without his consent or approval, his parents brought another baby boy home! If you have read anything about kings, you know how they protect their throne. And so it began; sibling rivalry with not one, but eventually two usurpers, to the throne of David—brothers Bob and Jim.

In high school, David thought he was average, but that was not true. David was smart. He just didn't know what smart looked like yet. He didn't have a yardstick with which to compare himself. He was nice looking, had a great personality that attracted people to him, and he knew how to get his mother to type his homework!

He wasn't encouraged to broaden his horizons. Now, you can learn anything on Google and YouTube. Use it to your advantage!

David was tenacious and focused. Even as a child. He was curious and wanted to learn things. David built a house—a two-story house—out of toothpicks, just to see if he could. He was a born leader. Leaders quite often are full of self-doubt. What makes them different, is they don't let that doubt stand in the way of their goals. Even though he lived just two doors down from the elementary school, he was rarely at school on time; but he could sing and did start his own band.

David was also kind and interested in people. He had the gift of giving you his full attention. He made a lot of mistakes. He would never hold a mistake against anyone. If you were trying; he was helping.

Children, this is David's legacy and your heritage. Be proud and confident. You are lucky!

SPINAL CORD INJURY STATISTICS

As of 2019, there were between 249,000 and 363,000 people living with spinal cord injuries in the U.S. Each year over 17,000 new cases join their ranks, primarily due to vehicle accidents, which account for almost 40% of all spinal injuries. Falls account for 31%; gunshot wounds, 13%; sports injuries, 8%; medical mishaps, 4%; and 3% by all other accidents. 39.5% of the total injured become paraplegic and 59.9% quadriplegic.

The vast majority of spinal cord injuries, 78%, are in males. Nineteen years old is the most frequent age of injury, two thirds of which are caused by diving accidents. Falls replace motorcycle injuries after the age of 43. First year medical expenses for quadriplegics start at $1,129,302. Lifetime costs are over 5 million. 77% are still unemployed after 10 years. 81% who survive the first 24 hours are still alive 10 years later. Only 30% have private insurance. Most return to their homes to be cared for by family.

This information is taken from the National Spinal Cord Injury Statistics Center at University of Alabama at Birmingham.

David VanGorder

· May 22, 1943 - September 26, 2019

" Daily expressing
gratitude
for what I have
instead of what I don't
have has given me
unlimited success and
happiness!

It's not what happens
to you... it's what you do
about it that makes all
the difference. **"**

Made in the USA
Columbia, SC
15 September 2021

44912090R00085